MICHELANN PARR / TERRY CAMPBELL

BALANCED

WEAVING THEORY INTO PRACTICE FOR SUCCESSFUL

LITERACY

INSTRUCTION IN READING, WRITING, AND TALK

ESSENTIALS

Pembroke Publishers Limited

© 2012 Pembroke Publishers
538 Hood Road
Markham, Ontario, Canada L3R 3K9
www.pembrokepublishers.com

Distributed in the U.S. by Stenhouse Publishers
480 Congress Street
Portland, ME 04101
www.stenhouse.com

We acknowledge the financial support of the Government of Canada through the Book Publishing Industry Development Program (BPIDP) for our publishing activities.

We acknowledge the assistance of the Government of Ontario through the Ontario Media Development Corporation's Ontario Book Initiative.

Library and Archives Canada Cataloguing in Publication

Parr, Michelann
    Balanced literacy essentials : weaving theory into practice for successful instruction in reading, writing, and talk / Michelann Parr & Terry Campbell.

Includes bibliographical references and index.
Issued also in electronic format.
ISBN 978-1-55138-275-3

    1. English language — Study and teaching (Elementary). 2. Literacy programs. I. Campbell, Terry, 1951–   II. Title.

LB1576.P355 2012   372.6'044   C2011-908365-5

eBook format ISBN 978-1-55138-837-3

Editor: Kate Revington
Cover Design: John Zehethofer
Typesetting: Jay Tee Graphics Ltd.

Printed and bound in Canada
9 8 7 6 5 4 3 2 1

MIX
Paper from responsible sources
FSC
www.fsc.org   FSC® C004071

CONTENTS

CHAPTER 1

The Art of Navigation in Teaching

It is this art [*navigation*] that drew me to love the sea at a very young age and that compelled me to challenge its treacherous waters all of my life and that made me navigate and follow the coast of parts of America . . .
— Samuel de Champlain, explorer extraordinaire, 1613

Leo Lionni's picture book *Frederick* has become a touchstone text for each of us. We both loved this book when we taught elementary students. When we shifted to teaching teacher candidates, we found it equally compelling. The text became one we wanted future teachers in our language and literacy course to know, to consider, and to "ponder deeply." The book's layers of meaning, its simple, evocative illustrations, and, above all, the memorable dreamer mouse, Frederick, make it fertile ground for thinking, feeling, questioning, and discussing — it doesn't matter whether the reader is 5 or 50. *Frederick* has sparked lively debate about what counts as "work," friendship, the value of the arts, the power of imagination, and the contributions to the group by those individuals who are "different." It is exactly the sort of text we champion the use of.

Although it appears to be straightforward, *Frederick* invariably stimulates strong reactions from our students. Teachers-to-be have voiced a wide range of opinions. One group wanted to "vote Frederick off the island," criticizing his laziness as a bad role model for children. Others admired his artistic nature and appreciated the role of dreamer. Initial responses are often revised after a second or third reading. *Frederick* is a book that is worth returning to and revisiting again and again — our definition of a "touchstone" text.

Touchstones

By *touchstone text*, a term coined by Lucy Calkins (1994), we are referring to all types of texts that are read, viewed, or experienced on multiple occasions for multiple purposes over time. These texts become part of the collective narrative of a classroom community.

A Line on Which to Hang Concerns and Understandings

In *The Girl with the Brown Crayon*, Vivian Gussin Paley recounts her experiences "doing Leo Lionni" in her Kindergarten class. Reeny, the student who inspired the title of Paley's book, identifies with Frederick: "that brown mouse seem to be just like me." Reeny is a Frederick-type of character — an artist, a poet, one who contributes something unique and valuable to the group.

Paley delved into Leo Lionni's books for the entire school year, creating conditions where "five or six year olds debate their concerns with as much fervor and insight as could any group of adults" (1997, p. 18). As they used Lionni's stories as a line on which to hang their concerns and growing understandings, the students' knowledge of character and social dynamics developed with astonishing depth.

This Kindergarten community became expert navigators of Lionni's texts — and day by day, they collaboratively navigated the world of literacy.

As navigators, literacy teachers and learners plan, direct, and travel their routes towards literacy, making use of multiple tools and texts to read their environment, chart their route, and adjust their sails when necessary, particularly if they feel part of their world is in jeopardy. They blend theory and practice, reception and expression of information through the language arts, and thinking, doing, and becoming in a seamless way. In Paley's Kindergarten classroom, all members of the community were free to read, write, and talk not simply about literal interpretations of Lionni, but far beyond, into the texts of their lives, their identities, and their places in the world.

So, what are the conditions that foster such engagement and enable students and teachers to grow into literacy? For us, the essentials for effective balanced literacy instruction include the following:

- knowing yourself within the context of your own literacy experiences, curriculum expectations, and the literacy outcomes you envision for your students (see Chapter 1)
- creating a classroom community that fosters respect for individual differences and makes it possible for students to take risks while feeling safe and supported (see Chapter 2)
- organizing your classroom through the effective establishment of literacy workshops, centres, and anchor charts (see Chapter 3)
- fostering constructive and accountable talk for learning and communication (see Chapter 4)
- using read-alouds to model the range of literate behaviors required of students who read, write, and talk with confidence (see Chapter 5)
- understanding reading as a complex process that involves multiple roles, responses, and levels of support (see Chapter 6)
- understanding writing in terms of purpose, pleasure, and multiple levels of support (see Chapter 7)
- using poetry to engage students in playing with and exploring language, both aloud and written (see Chapter 8)
- envisioning drama as a dynamic way of knowing that brings story and information to life (see Chapter 9)
- using traditional and digital storytelling as ways for students to create and share stories that matter to them (see Chapter 10)

So Many Questions to Ponder
One way to approach a story such as *Frederick* is to maintain a questioning stance about the author and illustrator. In this case, what was Leo Lionni's purpose when constructing the story? Why does he create a character that seems to refuse to work with the group as they busily prepare for winter? Why does he choose a small, brown mouse and use shades of grey with splashes of primary color in the scenery? Such uncomplicated illustrations, such a down-to-earth story, yet so many questions to ponder.

Of her memorable Kindergarten year, Paley (1997, p. 10) writes: "But what is really happening? Is it the contagious effect of one charismatic child's determination to celebrate a mouse as she celebrates herself? Or do I deliberately engineer this phenomenon because, without something entirely new and remarkable going on, I slip into a half-life? Each year I wait to be awakened by a Reeny, just as she has entered school looking for a Frederick, a something to ponder deeply and expand upon extravagantly."

In the text that follows, you are invited to reflect upon your literacy teaching — to determine "what is really happening" — and with, we hope, our help, to chart a course that leads your students in the direction they need and want to go.

Understanding Yourself as a Teacher of Language and Literacy

Consider how texts such as *Frederick* and experiences such as Lionni describes have shaped your identity as a teacher. Perhaps there have been times when your goals and those of the group (your colleagues, your family, your friends) were at odds. Perhaps the tensions were resolved through creative approaches — seeing things from a fresh perspective or in brighter colors. In part inspired by Frederick, we hope to offer you various inventive approaches — some new and some remarkable practices that deserve revisiting. An adventurous spirit, combined with creativity, is invaluable when considering, exploring, and ultimately navigating literacy essentials.

We recommend beginning with a good, long look at who you are and who you are becoming as a teacher. As teacher educators, we do this every autumn: along with the teacher candidates in our course, we question who and where we are as we embark on an eight-month adventure and travel beyond into the landscapes of literacy education.

Many of us, both present and future literacy educators, are equipped with the strategies and tools common to literate beings. Often, what we lack is an awareness of *how* we acquired them and the many influences, positive and negative, that have shaped who we are.

But teaching requires an awareness of who we are as literate beings and why we behave as we do. Our intuitive ideas about literacy — about listening, speaking, reading, writing, viewing, and representing — underlie our literacy teaching, our planning, and our interactions with students. Recognizing these implicit assumptions is critical to understanding; it helps us decide which ideas we need to set aside, to reconsider, to retain, and, above all, to call into question.

The following questions pertain to personal strengths and preferences. We invite you to consider them:

- Are your memories of literacy learning positive? Or are they negative?
- What is it that you have brought into your classroom?
- What are your strengths as a literate being? What are your needs?
- Are you comfortable speaking in large groups? Or, do you prefer small groups?
- Are you an active listener?
- Do you prefer to attend a lecture or read a book?
- Do you like to read? What do you like to read?
- Do you like to write? What do you like to write?
- Are you a critical viewer? Do you recognize the impact of music, lighting, camera angle?
- How do you prefer to represent your learning? Do you write songs or poetry? Do you draw or paint pictures?

If you picked up this book, you probably view the role of a teacher of language and literacy as going well beyond *covering* the curriculum in a way that prepares students for standardized testing. You likely appreciate that a well-rounded teacher of language and literacy teaches students in a way that recognizes who they are in multiple contexts, what they bring to the learning environment, and where they can go in the context of the classroom and beyond.

Teachers of language and literacy may look to metaphors that allow them to envision their role in a meaningful and holistic way (Lakoff & Johnson, 1980; Massengill Shaw & Mahlios, 2011). For example, some teachers view themselves as jugglers, ever aware of the number of balls they have to work with (e.g., differentiation, parents, and school board directives), trying to ensure that the balls are always in the air and that no one ball is dropped long enough to harm the overall juggling act — ultimately, a child's learning. Some teachers see themselves as circus ringleaders fully aware of the multiple rings they are expected to keep watch over: the ring of curriculum, the ring of accountability, the ring of children's strengths and needs, and so on. Their task is to coordinate the rings into one show and to ensure that the class is entertaining and worth coming back to tomorrow. And then some teachers are lighthouse keepers. They have a long view on curriculum and see the big picture; they have good sightlines and can see things from both within and outside. They offer a safe haven for students as they negotiate rocky shorelines.

Teachers may also look to real life and fiction for role models to inspire them. For example, consider Anne Sullivan, Helen Keller's teacher, or Erin Gruwel, whose story is covered in the film *Freedom Writers*. Fictional role models might range from Jane Eyre and Albus Dumbledore (in the Harry Potter series) to English professor John Keating in *Dead Poets Society*, Yoda in Star Wars, and LouAnne Johnson in *Dangerous Minds*.

How do you envision your role as a teacher of language and literacy?
- Do you look to a real role model, perhaps one profiled in books or films?
- Do you look to a fictional role model?
- Do you use a particular text to guide your overall philosophy and interaction with students (e.g., *Frederick* by Leo Lionni or "The Starfish" by Loren Eisley)?
- Or, do you reach for a metaphor to help you explain and understand your role?

Reflecting upon Your Language and Literacy Block

In today's classrooms, between 25 and 50 percent of a school day is allocated to the teaching of language and literacy. This amount of time can often be overwhelming, particularly for teachers in a new classroom or a new grade. We often wrestle with questions such as these:
- Where do I start?
- What do I do with an hour or more language and literacy block?
- How do I fit it all in? Is it even possible?
- How do I assess and evaluate?
And most important,
- How do I ensure that all my students meet with success?

In order to get started as a teacher in general or as a teacher of a new grade, or to challenge yourself so as not to "slip into a half-life" as Paley (1997, p. 10) dreads, consider adopting the role of navigator as a literacy learner and teacher. This orientation is characterized by a sense of adventure. As you embark on your journey, you need an open mind that relishes risk-taking, a willingness to question and consider closely, and a framework of dimensions, or guiding questions, to help you chart your course and plan an engaging program (see pages 10–12). We begin with an examination of what you currently do and believe as a teacher of language and literacy.

Take some time to think about your language and literacy block as it stands right now. Consider the following questions:

Other Metaphors for Teachers
Teacher candidates and colleagues have also proposed these metaphors:
- orchestra conductor
- artist whose classroom is the canvas
- director on a film set
- door
- a light, as in a "flood of illumination"

1. What are you doing well?
   - Make a list of the strengths of your language and literacy block. These might include resources, student responses, and long-range plans.
2. Are you balancing the language strands and support along the continuum?
   - You don't need to include everything in every lesson. That's the beauty of longer-range planning — you can see how over time the various dimensions can be addressed.
3. Do you have students who show particular strengths in specific dimensions? Where are the gaps?
   - When looking for gaps, try to think of a student who might have benefited from that particular gap being filled.
4. Do you need more strategies — or do you need to use your current strategies more effectively?
   - Identify and begin with what you're good at and gradually add to your repertoire. Using 10 strategies well is far better than doing 20 poorly.
5. How can you maintain your sanity and make constructive changes to your program?
   - To keep everything manageable, try one new strategy every two weeks.
   - Keep a log or journal to identify student responses, consequences — positive and negative — and outcomes. Repeat the same process again and again, until you have filled as many gaps as possible.
   - Maintain a focus on your students' needs — it will keep you motivated.
   - Keep in mind that the goal is to allow students to use their strengths not as something to fall into but as a tool to push them to grow on the edge of their comfort zones in their areas of greatest need.

The Language and Literacy Block: Adopting the Role of Navigator

As you reflect upon your language and literacy block, and the outcomes/goals you have for students, you may have many questions. We have organized the most common questions we hear from novice teachers into a framework that includes instructional, individual, and real-world dimensions. While you may view this framework as overwhelming, we urge you to work through the dimensions. They provide a theory-woven-into-practice way of conceptualizing the teaching of reading, writing, and talk in today's classroom.

The dimensions can be addressed in a variety of ways: you could take a holistic perspective, where you take a cursory glance at the big picture; you could work through the dimensions one at a time, beginning with what you've identified as your strength; or you could review the framework and choose the dimension that you feel needs most attention. Our goal is to get you thinking about your language and literacy block and how, through reflection, planning, and re-visioning, you can meet the needs of all learners in the classroom.

Please keep in mind that the framework is simply a starting point and can be adapted to meet your personal needs, the needs of your school, or the needs of a school district. (A reproducible framework for long-term planning begins on page 133.)

Literacy Essential 1: For your literacy journey in the classroom, adopt the adventurous orientation of a navigator, critically aware of personal strengths, formative influences, and dimensions that need to be considered.

Navigating the Dimensions Involved in Teaching Language and Literacy

The Instructional Dimension: *Constructing learning experiences using what are traditionally referred to as the six language arts, texts of many types and formats, multiple levels of support, and diverse teaching/learning strategies*

Six Language Arts

LISTENING:

☐ How do I structure opportunities (e.g., large-group, small-group, teacher, peer) for students to listen for multiple purposes (e.g., to learn, to demonstrate learning, to collaborate, to reflect)? How do I provide explicit instruction on how to be an effective listener?

SPEAKING:

☐ What opportunities (e.g., large-group, small-group, teacher, peer) do I provide for students to talk for multiple purposes (e.g., to learn, to demonstrate learning, to collaborate, to reflect)?

☐ How do I provide explicit instruction on how to be an effective speaker?

READING:

☐ How do I ensure that students have access to a range of written texts (e.g., literary, content, multimedia) in the classroom (e.g., teacher-selected and self-selected)?

☐ Are they given explicit strategies to navigate print text?

WRITING:

☐ How do I encourage students to write for a variety of purposes (e.g., to inform, to entertain, to reflect, to communicate) in a variety of text types (e.g., poetic, story, expository)?

VIEWING:

☐ How do I ensure that students have multiple opportunities to view, discuss, and closely examine texts of many types (e.g., picture books, memoirs/biographies, journal entries, performances, posters, media including documentaries, newscasts)?

REPRESENTING:

☐ How do I encourage students to create texts of many types (e.g., experiential texts through drama and storytelling, posters, media, digital texts)?

Texts of Many Types and Formats

ORAL TEXTS:

☐ How do I make oral texts (e.g., read-alouds, teacher–student, student–student, formal/informal) valued and critical sites for learning in the classroom?

MULTIMEDIA TEXTS:

☐ How do I teach students how to navigate (e.g., decode and create) a variety of multimedia texts (e.g., media, digital, picture, experiential)?

TECHOLOGY-MEDIATED TEXTS:

☐ What instructional technologies do I offer as supports in the acquisition of literacy (e.g., text-to-speech, speech-to-text technology, audio-texts)?

MULTIPLE LEVELS OF TEXTS:

☐ Are texts at a variety of reading levels provided? How are these organized?

☐ How do students access these texts?

STUDENT CHOICE OF TEXTS:

☐ Do I encourage student choice of text in the classroom, recognizing that texts of all types can be used in reading instruction?

LITERARY TEXTS:

☐ Do literary texts reflect the strengths, needs, and interests of my students?

CONTENT/INFORMATION TEXTS:

☐ Are content/information texts appropriate to the strengths, needs, and interests of my students?

☐ Are they organized in a way that facilitates student reading and acquisition of content?

OTHER:

Teaching/Learning Strategies

PROVIDING A CONTINUUM OF SUPPORT:

☐ How do I provide support to learners?

☐ Do I incorporate modelling and demonstration, using a balance of explicit instruction and thinking aloud? Do I incorporate interactive strategies that share instructional processes with students?

☐ Do I gradually release responsibility to students by offering a full continuum of support (e.g., making use of modelled, shared, interactive, guided, and independent levels of support)?

CHOOSING DIVERSE INSTRUCTIONAL STRATEGIES:

☐ How do instructional strategies reflect the strengths and needs of learners, the classroom context, and the goals of instruction?

USING DIVERSE STUDENT GROUPINGS (e.g., independent, small/large group):

☐ How do I use grouping strategies in the classroom to enhance instruction?

CHOOSING ORGANIZATIONAL STRUCTURES (e.g., anchor charts, workshops, literacy centres):

☐ What structures, rituals, and routines that enhance organization and learning are in place in the classroom?

USING DIVERSE ASSESSMENT TOOLS (e.g., checklist, conference, rubric, negotiated success criteria, portfolio):

☐ How do I ensure that assessment strategies are closely related to instructional strategies?
☐ How do I ensure that assessment incorporates feedback for learning and growth as well as evaluation for reporting and accountability purposes?

The Individual Dimension: *Shaping our teaching by taking into account how individuals learn and navigate texts of all types*

MULTIPLE INTELLIGENCES (Gardner, 1999):

☐ What types of opportunities do I structure to allow students to learn and demonstrate learning through their strengths and dominant intelligences (e.g., linguistic, logical-mathematical, spatial, bodily-kinesthetic, musical, intrapersonal, interpersonal, naturalist)?
☐ How do I ensure that students are aware of their strengths and needs?
☐ How do I encourage students to use their strengths to work on their needs?
☐ How does my overall program or plan for my language and literacy block reflect balance from a multiple intelligences perspective?

WAYS OF KNOWING:

☐ How do I recognize the diversity of ways of knowing in the classroom?
☐ Can I identify the students who learn best by listening, observing, doing/constructing/investigating, reflecting on experience, and thinking abstractly?
☐ Do I plan activities that allow students to know "something" through their dominant way of knowing, always providing opportunities for them to know through other ways?
☐ How does my overall program or plan for my language and literacy block reflect balance in terms of these ways of knowing?

WAYS OF BEING (CULTURE/FAMILY CHARACTERISTICS):

☐ How can I develop an awareness of the diversity of families in my classroom (e.g., language spoken in the home, extended families)?
☐ What languages are used in the home? What purposes do these languages serve?
☐ What cultural beliefs, values, and norms do students and families bring to the classroom? How can I ensure that each of these is valued in the classroom?
☐ Have I considered the economic demands placed on families by the school and my program? (Examples: purchase of supplies, field trips).
☐ How can I enhance the home–school connection and build habits for lifelong family engagement?

The Real-World Dimension: *Navigating and building bridges between the classroom and the realities of every-day life in the 21st century*

LOOKING AT THE FAMILIAR IN FRESH, CRITICAL WAYS:

☐ How do I provide opportunities for students to dig below the surface of texts of many types and formats?
☐ How do I encourage students to identify, work with, and create a variety of text structures (e.g., experiential, advertising, website, textbook, poetic, expository, digital) for real-world purposes?

CLOSELY CONSIDERING MULTIPLE VIEWPOINTS OR PERSPECTIVES:

☐ Am I willing to set aside my own perspectives and plans to follow the lead of the students?

- How do I encourage students to consider issues and texts from perspectives that differ from their own?
- How do they recognize points of view, omissions, and multiple perspectives?

TRAVELLING PURPOSEFULLY IN THE WORLD OF TEXT:

- How do students explore authors' and illustrators' decisions with regard to such things as what to write, how to write, how to illustrate, how to represent character and dialogue, and the effects that each of these has on meaning and relationships within the text?
- How do I encourage them to make connections to previous voyages with texts and other travellers?

CHARTING NEW COURSES:

- How do I encourage students to move beyond simply reading, experiencing, and interpreting texts into making the world a better place?
- How do they use texts of all types to transform their worlds and those of their peers?

CHAPTER 2

A Community for Learning Success

Building a sense of membership in a community helps students overcome anxiety and gain positive self-efficacy; it also enhances learning and understanding.
— David Booth

Creating a community at the classroom level is fundamental to literacy learning. The research is clear that we learn to be literate *with* others, not in isolation. The social nature of reading and writing requires that students learn to read and write inside a community. The related language arts of speaking, listening, viewing, and representing — all part of literacy — are embedded in social activities. Think of the schoolyard games where the theme is a new pop song or a famous celebrity, the great debates that take place after contemporary books have been read, or the discussions of what to buy (or not) as a result of media campaigns. None of these takes place in isolation, but they do take place in contexts of respect, care, and trust, often within groups of the students' own choosing.

So, how can we bring what we know about such informal groups into the formal group of a classroom?

As in viable informal groups, fostering a community of literacy learners requires respect, care, and trust. A respectful classroom includes everyone, regardless of individual differences. In a classroom where trust is established, students feel that their voices are valued and respected. A culture of care supports students as they explore their identities and roles in groups, and create connections beyond the walls of the school. Teaching goes beyond planning meaningful and authentic opportunities. Effective teachers ensure that students feel welcome and valued, and feel supported and encouraged as they grow and learn socially, emotionally, and cognitively.

Developing a Vision of Community

"Community, not curriculum, is where many of our improvement efforts now need to be focused."
— Andy Hargreaves

Ideal classroom communities are characterized by a common set of values, expectations, routines, and rituals. The classrooms are spaces where members share interests, adopt roles, and work collaboratively to achieve common goals. Yet students will not be at the same level, reading and writing the same texts, or doing the same thing. On the contrary, students will likely be doing different things at different times, always working towards the common goal. Creating a classroom community enables you to provide a common and predictable experience that allows all of your students to feel connected, relate positively to others, and solve problems respectfully.

Building a community is something to plan for before the school doors open in September, but being flexible is important. While you will arrive prepared, an idea in mind or a curriculum to consider, ultimately, your students will define your community and your areas of focus. Part of your role as a teacher is to take the children from where they are to where they can be: something that cannot be accomplished by teaching curriculum in isolation of community. Classroom communities are dynamic and organic; they change and evolve as children change and grow and as you change and grow. One year, you might have a group of children who are interested in studying Leo Lionni (as Paley's group did); another year, you might have a group of children who are particularly interested in digital and media literacies. One day, you might have children who are fascinated by the first snowfall, while another day, your students have to be outside chasing frogs as a shared and community experience.

Have a plan for getting to know your students. Perhaps you will adopt a range of energizers so that you and your students will get to know one another's names (see pages 20 to 21 for some of our favorite community-building activities). In the first week of school, focus on getting to know your students' strengths, needs (academic, social, and emotional), learning styles, multiple intelligences, and so on. Envision manageable routines that will ultimately lead to a classroom plan for behavior and respect for individual differences. The classroom expectations anchor chart on page 18 provides a model.

You can build community in concrete ways. Find something that will provoke discussion on the theme. You might pose questions: *How can we make our classroom community a caring space? What do we bring to our classroom? How can we work cooperatively?* For younger children, you may want to work with a picture book, image, or DVD that deals with a specific related issue (e.g., teasing, individual differences, doing your best). For older children, use of a picture book, a news story, a controversial film, website, a poster, or a TV advertisement (respect, rights and responsibilities, questioning) may be appropriate. Whatever you select should fit well with the vision of community you have for your classroom.

To demonstrate, we have selected two texts that have worked well for us, but there are many more with similar topics and themes that work equally as well. Beyond the suggested lessons, use the texts referenced in the chapter as starting points for conversation, community building, and the development of classroom expectations. These can be used for shared reading and oral language activities. Return to these books on multiple occasions throughout the year (and search for many others) each time you see an opportunity for conversation. Students can often relate far easier to characters in texts than they can explain what is happening in their own lives.

Lesson Plan 1 for Creating a Community

Selected Text: *Chrysanthemum* by Kevin Henkes

Chrysanthemum is a great book for beginning the school year. Chrysanthemum is a girl whose parents thought she was perfect, so they gave her what they considered to be a perfect name. Chrysanthemum loved her name. And then she started school . . . .

Exploring Names

Introduce the *Chrysanthemum* picture book (or DVD). First, ask students to look at the cover. Prompt them to make predictions about story theme. Activate prior knowledge by inviting them to share what they know about teasing — almost every child has been teased at least once. Ask: "How did the teasing make you feel?" If beginning with a DVD, as is available for *Chrysanthemum*, let students know that you will also be reading the book so that they can make comparisons.

Identify words that students might have difficulty understanding (e.g., *appreciate, dreadful, begrudging, envious, discontented*). Record students' questions, predictions, and wonder statements about the selected text on a class chart.

Understanding characters, envisioning community

Play the DVD first, if there is one; otherwise, give a first read-aloud of the book.

Use questions that support students as they make connections, come up with questions of their own, and react to the story. Ask: "Why do you think the author named Chrysanthemum after a flower? What do you notice about the characters? Do the pictures tell us how Chrysanthemum is really feeling? Can you relate to Chrysanthemum? How do you think students in the classroom should feel?"

Support students as they discuss and explore the range of emotions Chrysanthemum experiences throughout the story. Encourage them to raise questions or offer comments that reflect their ways of being and their cultural models — these may include issues related to power, history, friendship, and culture. For example:

> Where is the classroom teacher? Why didn't the teacher do something about Victoria, Jo, and Rita when they were teasing Chrysanthemum? Why were the other students so mean to Chrysanthemum?

> I think the other mice teased Chrysanthemum because they wished their name was as long and as unique as hers.

Share with the students your vision of classroom community as a place where students feel safe and valued. Relate this vision to emotions experienced by Chrysanthemum. Discuss the differences in the approaches of the regular classroom teacher and of Ms. Twinkle, and outline what your approach will be.

Affirming that names are special, individuals unique

Provide students with large sheets of heavyweight paper. Ask them to write, paint, stamp, or cut-and-paste their names onto the paper, decorating with centre supplies (e.g., glitter, feathers, pasta, rice, sand). Observe and discuss how nobody decorated their names the same just as nobody in the classroom is the same. Talk to students about how special their names are. Tell your name story (where your name comes from, what it means, how it is special), and encourage students to share what they know about their names.

Encountering the Dynamics of Bullying

Introduce *Hooway for Wodney Wat* by asking students to make predictions about what they think the story might be about. Record students' questions, predictions, and wonder statements about the selected text on a class chart.

First encounter with the theme

Read aloud a powerful text that is relevant to students' lives and will provide a place for them to explore their understanding of self and the world. Our recommendation is *Hooway for Wodney Wat*.

Lesson Plan 2 for Creating a Community

Selected Text: *Hooway for Wodney Wat* by Helen Lester

A rat has trouble pronouncing the letter *r*. Teased, he is rendered shy and nervous. But then, big, mean, smart Camilla the Capybara arrives in the classroom. Capitalizing on Wodney's mispronunciation of *r* and Camilla's new student status, Wodney and his classmates play Simon Says. Camilla, feeling rather bullied, decides to leave the school.

Use questions that support students as they make connections, ask further questions, and react to the story. Ask: "Whose voices are heard? Whose voices are not heard? How does the use of language tell us about the characters? For example, what does Camilla's use of language tell us about her? Why are things the way they are? How can we change them? Why did the author make Wodney a rat and Camilla a capybara, a very large rodent? How does the text depict individual differences? How do the characters' words demonstrate who is stronger and more powerful? Are the pictures consistent with the characters' words?"

Considering roles and perspectives

Introduce and define the four roles we often encounter in bullying situations (Christensen, 2004; Laman, 2006). Help students to connect these roles to those they encounter in real life.

Ask students to think about the story and identify who they consider to be a victim, an ally, a bystander, or a bully. Record thoughts on cue cards and attach to a chart accessible during the read-aloud.

In a second reading, encourage students to ask questions about the roles and revise initial thoughts throughout the reading. Add cue cards if students now see the roles differently.

Follow up with a discussion of roles and how the roles shifted throughout the story. Ask whether Wodney was a victim or a bully. Invite students to make connections to their own lives. Have they ever been an ally, a bystander, a victim, or a bully?

Especially during multiple readings, students might raise questions that relate to power, history, friendship, and culture. For example:

> Why didn't the teacher do something about Camilla when she was bullying?
> Why would the teacher let Camilla yell out answers without raising her hand?
> How did the other rodents feel when they were bullied by Camilla?
> Did they think about how they treated Wodney?
> Why didn't the other rodents tell Camilla about Wodney?

They might offer comments such as these:

> *Student 1:* In the end, Wodney thought he was a hero. His voice was louder and he thought he was saving the day.
> *Student 2:* I think the other rodents used Wodney. Today, he thinks he is a hero but what will happen tomorrow when Camilla is not there anymore? Will they start teasing him and bullying him again?
> *Student 3:* I don't think it was fair for them to run Camilla out of town. It was her first day at a new school. Maybe she was nervous, maybe she didn't want to be teased about how big she was so she used her size to be a bully instead. Everyone knows that bullies don't usually get teased.

Small-group discussions

Remind students of questions that were recorded during the first and second read-alouds.

Group students in a way that maximizes participation and exploration of key topics.

Encourage students to focus on answering the questions raised during the read-aloud, recording their responses for future reference.

During the small-group discussions, encourage students to monitor their discussions by putting a star beside the questions that generate the most talk. For example:

> Why do bullies act like this?
> Why can't they be nice?
> Why does the teacher look mean when trying to listen to Wodney? It's not Wodney's fault.
> Why would the other rodents tease him like that?
> Why did Camilla leave? Didn't she understand it was just a game?*

Partner/Triad response to guided prompts

Prepare a list of prompts for use by students. For example:

> What is important to remember about this book?
> What surprised you about this book?
> From your own life list one or two writing topics that connect with the story.
> Why do you think people should or should not read this story?
> Write one or two statements about someone whose point of view is (or is not) represented in the story. Or, write as a character.

Group students in a way that will promote participation and exploration of key topics. Allow 15 to 20 minutes for discussion, monitoring student engagement and adjusting time accordingly.

Students might respond to the prompts through writing, oral recording, or oral presentation. Here is how one student responded in character as Wodney:

> Don't you know this isn't my fault? Don't you know that I am working hard to fix my r's? Don't you know that every time you tease me, you make me feel so very alone?

Whole-class response and problem-solving

The whole class engages in a conversation about the story, paying particular attention to the questions raised in previous encounters and the following questions, if not already on the students' list: *How might our weaknesses also be strengths? What does it mean to be a new kid at school? Is it appropriate to bully a bully?*

Prompt students to use information from the text and previous sessions to collectively select one illustration or quotation that best represents their learning from this story. Encourage them to make this part of their audit trail, historical trail, or learning wall (see page 20).

Discuss with students school-wide solutions to bullying on the schoolyard (e.g., peacemakers, character education, social skills training).

Negotiating Classroom Expectations

Classroom expectations will reflect the personality of the teacher and the community of learners. Some teachers and classes prefer a short statement such as the Golden Rule (Do unto others as you would have them do unto you); other teachers negotiate a set of explicit guidelines for classroom behavior. Stories that are set in a classroom, such as *Chrysanthemum* and *Hooway for Wodney Wat*, can be used as a springboard for discussion. Students can discuss what they liked about the classroom in the story and what they didn't like, and brainstorm how they expect to be treated in their classroom.

As students gain experience with school, discussions can be more complex, and students can be engaged at higher levels. Some teachers ask students to brainstorm independently the optimal conditions for them to learn and thrive in a classroom ("What would the classroom have to be like in order for you to do your best work and enjoy school?"); they then compile these conditions and review them with students, gradually and collaboratively shaping a set of expectations similar to those negotiated by the junior class below. When expectations for behavior are made explicit in the classroom, students know exactly what is expected of them and how their behavior affects their own learning and that of their peers. Many teachers find that students are also more likely to meet these expectations when they know that they will be held accountable not only by the teacher but by their peers.

Orally negotiating classroom expectations and then writing them up in anchor-chart form help build ownership of expectations for behavior and establish criteria for success. The anchor chart "Our Classroom Expectations" was negotiated by a junior-level Social Skills class in the Nipissing-Parry Sound Catholic District School Board.

Anchor Chart: The Three Rs
Respect yourself.
Respect others.
Respect this place.

Our Classroom Expectations
In our classroom,
- We are all welcome and have a right to feel safe and secure.
- We have a right to learn.
- We are all worthwhile and have something unique to offer others.
- We have a right to speak and be listened to.
- We have a right to be treated with dignity and respect, and to feel good about ourselves.
- We have a right to personal space. We do not touch each other.
- We have a right to personal property. We ask each others' permission to touch or borrow things, and we return them as we found them.
- We use appropriate language. We don't allow put-downs, name-calling, criticisms, insults or swearing.

Establishing What Is Fair

All texts that are used in this chapter — metaphorical, video, read-aloud, and discussion — focus on students in a classroom getting to know themselves and learning how to respect their individual differences in the classroom and beyond. Students need to accept and view individual differences in a way that goes past tolerance. Everyone has strengths and everyone has needs; no two of us are alike. Students can discuss what characters need to succeed in the classroom and make connections to themselves. Frederick is a dreamer, often appearing not to work. Chrysanthemum is bright, bubbly, and eager for school. Wodney is shy and has difficulty pronouncing certain letters. Each story character has different needs to succeed — essentially, each one needs to feel safe and valued.

Regardless of the grade level taught, these lessons can allow entry into a discussion of what we all need to succeed and an agreement that what is fair is not always equal; instead, fairness is when we all get what we need to succeed.

In addition, texts such as these often allow students to step outside their own realities and walk around in the heads of characters. Sometimes what they cannot see in their own lives becomes clear and often less threatening when encountered in a story. Story, even news story, characters and situations can be talked about openly without violating confidence or centring out students in a way that we would never talk about the "real" situations.

Forging Relationships with Families

Knowing when and how to elicit the support and input of parents and caregivers is important. Doing this is particularly useful when we are trying to get to know our students at the beginning of an academic year. Over the school year, consider ways of forging relationships with parents, families, other teachers, and community librarians to create communities of readers and writers. Several sound ways to get to know students and their families follow.

Give open-ended prompts that stimulate discussions with families and caregivers: *Tell me about your child's language and literacy development, beginning with their first words, the stories they love to hear over and over again, or the songs you have heard them singing.* Alternatively, provide structured questions such as these: *What are your child's strengths? What does your child like to read? What was your child's favorite reading time like?* If using a print questionnaire, be aware of the diversity of your families. Be sure to offer opportunities for face-to-face conferencing or an interpreter when necessary.

Make a River of Reading to discover more about children's out-of-school reading: provide the outline of a river on a sheet of paper, and invite children and their families to create a river of all the reading they engage with over one weekend. Sample instructions:
- Draw, stick on, or write about anything you read over the weekend . . . comics, magazines, hockey cards, books, DVD cases, computer games, chocolate wrappers . . . anything and everything!
- Invite your parent(s), brothers or sisters, or anyone else at home to list their own reading and write their names next to their bits.
- Bring your river to school so that you can share all the reading you have done.

As a teacher, you may want to share your own reading over a weekend (e.g., magazines, recipes, labels, books). Invite other teachers in the school to contribute. Post the Rivers down the hallway. (Source: Cremin, Mottram, Collins, & Powell, 2011)

Elicit name stories that require children and parents to respond to questions such as these: *What's your full name? Were you named after someone? What does your name mean? What names did your parents consider before deciding on the one you have? Why did they choose your name? What is your name's country of origin?* (For example, *Ivan* has Russian origins.) *What is your nickname? How did you get that nickname? If you could change your name, what would you name yourself?*

Make families aware of classroom expectations by sending them home with students. If appropriate, families should also know the consequences for not meeting the expectations. Encourage parents to discuss the expectations with their child, commenting on similarities and differences between home and school expectations.

More Strategies for Building a Learning Community

Here are some ideas that you can either adopt to extend your repertoire of community-building strategies or relate to your current practice.

Create an audit trail, a historical trail, or a learning wall. No matter what it's called, keep a record of learning and community events that take place in the classroom over the course of the year. This record often encompasses goals established and met. The format that the record of learning takes can be negotiated with students. It may be a series of posters created by the students, a series of book jackets posted sequentially as each touchstone text is used in the classroom, or even a set of calendars prepared month by month that show the passage of time and key events. The audit trail, historical trail, or learning wall is visible not only to students in the classroom, but also to families and visitors to the classroom.

Establish unifying images for the classroom. Introduce something like a theme song or poem or focused author study or hero at the beginning of the year. The class can ponder deeply the text, author worth returning to (e.g., Leo Lionni), or hero (e.g., Terry Fox) all year. With the students, determine a symbol that represents the collection of personalities that make up the class or a mascot. This activity can be a powerful way to build and sustain community throughout the school year. The unifying images become the basis for artwork and writing to post in the room, for discussions and dramatic role-play, and above all, for identity and community building.

Play the Web of Names game. Students stand or sit in a circle. A ball of yarn is tossed from one to another, with the name of the student who is to receive the ball called out each time. Once all students' names have been called, students must untangle the web by reversing the calling of names. As comfort in the classroom grows and an inclusive community is built, this web can be used to highlight strengths or good things students have noted about one another.

Make a name wave. Students stand in a circle. In this cumulative game, the whole class is involved in repeating the name and action of one student at a time. The first student says his or her name and does an action. This name along with the action is repeated by the person to the right and then the next until the name and action return to the originating student. The next student then says his or her name and provides an action.

Community Building from the First Day

Here are two memories of almost perfect first days of school with new students.

Neighborhood or Nature Walk: Terry Campbell

In the afternoon, once the indoor chores (e.g., attendance and seating arrangements), were finished, I read my Grade 4 class Byrd Baylor's classic,

Everybody Needs a Rock, which lists the ten rules for finding a perfect rock. We then went outside into the neighborhood right around the school to find our own perfect rocks. My only rule (about choosing a rock) was that it had to fit easily in the hand. I'm afraid that my rules for going out were copious: lining up down the right-hand side of the stairs, going outside in an orderly way (this is not the same as recess!), walking in pairs on the sidewalk, moving to the right for neighbors (especially the elderly ones), and so on. I explained that they had to be able to walk as a group in a safe, orderly way, because I had lots of exciting places to go with them this year — the public library, the arts centre, the YMCA, skating rinks — all within walking distance. We returned safely, labelled our rocks, displayed them in the Science station, and investigated rocks and minerals later in the month. We finished our day with the traditional Irish song "Tell My Ma" (Rankin Family version), and posted it on the Music board. Before the students left for home, we reviewed the day and I handed out newsletters about the exciting year ahead of us. That first day everyone went home (down the right-hand side of the stairs!) smiling, some still singing.

Rainbow Fish School: Michelann Parr

A good school year for me always begins with a good story. I want to start off the year right and I want my students to understand what life in my Grade 1 classroom is all about. We begin the day by reading *Rainbow Fish* by Marcus Phister and discuss how each one of us is special and has unique strengths; from there, we discuss sharing in the classroom. I have prepared in advance a large fish for each student to cut out (which allows me to assess this skill) and an envelope of colored scales for each student (e.g., Thomas's scales are blue; Mariska gets sparkly scales). Students wander around the classroom until they have exchanged a scale with every other student in the classroom, saying hello, and chatting briefly. Once their envelopes are full of multi-colored scales, they return to the tables where they cut out their fish and begin to glue their scales on. Student are each given a googly eye to finish their creation and asked to write their name on their original scale. All fish are hung in the classroom for all to see as a reminder of our uniqueness and ability to share.

Literacy Essential 2: A classroom community founded on clear routines, knowledge of students, respect, and conscious use of community-building activities makes possible the effective teaching of literacy curriculum.

Community-Building Texts of Many Types

Literature and texts of many types, when read aloud or experienced, can support community building and meaningful social skills discussions when structured by the teacher. These opportunities support students as they try to better understand themselves and their world.

Illustrated fiction texts

Oh, the Places You'll Go! by Dr. Seuss

Scaredy Squirrel by Mélanie Watt
If You Find a Rock by Peggy Christian
Do unto Otters: A Book About Manners by Laurie Keller
Chrysanthemum by Kevin Henkes
All the Colors of the Earth by Sheila Hamanaka
The Dot and *Ish* by Peter Reynolds
First Day Jitters by Julie Danneberg
Stone Soup by Jon J. Muth
The Three Questions by Jon J. Muth
Ruby the Copycat by Peggy Rathman
Hooway for Wodney Wat by Helen Lester
The Name Jar by Yangsook Choi
Marianthe's Story: Painted Words and Spoken Memories by Aliki
Miss Nelson Is Missing by Harry Allard and James Marshall
The Giving Tree by Shel Silverstein
Enemy Pie by Derek Munsen

Multiple intelligences and learning differences

Frederick by Leo Lionni
Three Pebbles and a Song by Eileen Spinelli
A Walk in the Rain with a Brain by Edward Hallowell
Through the Cracks by Carolyn Solomon
Thank You, Mr. Falker by Patricia Polacco
Crow Boy by Taro Yashima

Illustrated information texts

We Are All Born Free: The Universal Declaration of Human Rights in Pictures by Amnesty International
Listen to the Wind: The Story of Dr. Greg & Three Cups of Tea by Greg Mortensen and Susan L. Roth
Every Human Has Rights by Mary Robinson (National Geographic)
Terry Fox: A Story of Hope by Maxine Trottier
Courage and Compassion: Ten Canadians Who Made a Difference by Rona Arat

Non-print media

Chrysanthemum (DVD Scholastic)
Do unto Otters (DVD Scholastic)
The Tale of Despereaux (film; directed by Sam Fell and Robert Stevenhagen)
The Miraculous Journey of Edward Tulane (audio CD and website: www.edwardtulane.com)
Swimmy and More Classic Leo Lionni Stories (DVD)
Terry (DVD; the Terry Fox story from Knightscove Studio)
Terry Fox and the Terry Fox Foundation: www.terryfox.org/Foundation/index.html

Dear Families,

Re: Getting to Know Your Child

As your child's new teacher, I would appreciate help in getting to know your child better. Any insights you share with me through the survey below will help me tailor my instruction to better serve your child. Feel free to discuss the survey with your child. You are welcome to use extra sheets of paper and attach pictures. You and I are partners in your child's learning!

What is your child's attitude towards school?

☐ Very enthusiastic
☐ Positive; likes school
☐ Indifferent; no strong likes or dislikes
☐ Negative; does not like school

Describe any special interests, talents, or strengths your child has.

How often does your child read at home? What are your child's favorite stories or texts to read or to hear someone read aloud?

Does your child take part in any activities or hobbies — for example, dance, music, drama, or sports? Tell me about them.

What do you think your child would like to accomplish this year?

Please share any additional information you would like me to know about your child.

Pembroke Publishers © 2012 *Balanced Literacy Essentials* by Michelann Parr, Terry Campbell. ISBN 978-1-55138-275-3

CHAPTER 3

Literacy Workshops: Where Theory and Practice Meet

You walk through the door and are transported to a place where children and literacy can blossom. The space isn't big, but every inch is being utilized thoughtfully. There is a classroom library in the corner with labeled baskets of books and some cool chairs that make you want to curl up and read. On the walls are charts made by the students and teacher that show what they've been learning. There's an area for whole-group teaching and a separate space with a table for small-group teaching. This room is a place where the teacher works to meet the needs of all students in a variety of instructional settings, . . . It's a place where children are valued.

— Debbie Diller (2008, p. 1)

Creating a classroom where literacy thrives in the buzz of a workshop atmosphere is where theory and practice meet. Children learn by doing. Workshops for teaching and learning, where teacher-directed mini-lessons are combined with active learning centres set up for independent practice and success, address the ways children learn through play and work. Teachers enjoy and excel in their teaching when they have the opportunities to express their personal traits and creativity.

[C]reative practice is seen as a product of the dynamic interplay between the teacher's personal qualities, the pedagogy they adopt and the ethos developed in the class and school. A number of key features of creative practice: curiosity, making connections, autonomy and ownership as well as originality. (Cremin, 2009, p. 36)

Creative Practice

The key features of creative practice are the very characteristics we want to foster in our students. Creating the conditions for active learning for all of your students allows you, as a teacher, to apply what you know theoretically in ways that match your learners' needs. Is it a lot of work? Yes, but doing so makes your teaching more interesting, energizing, and effective, and the learning more engaging.

We know that classroom instruction requires a delicate balance of whole-group, small-group, and one-on-one instruction, but we often find this difficult to deliver. Sometimes, we can't quite determine what the rest of the class is doing while we are otherwise engaged. Key questions:

- When I'm working with small groups, is the rest of the class engaged productively in meaningful and authentic learning? How do I get them there?
- How do I keep track of this learning? How do I assess this learning?
- *And most important:* How do I manage this classroom? How can I ensure that my students work independently and collaboratively in a way that enables me to work with small groups and even individual students?

Variation Within Workshops
Literacy workshops blend and naturally integrate a variety of instructional practices to facilitate student success. They make use of a full continuum of support (from modelling or demonstration to independent practice). They provide teachers with opportunities to balance work with individual students, small groups of students, and the whole class.

These questions have no quick answers, and the classroom solution cannot be described through a recipe or formula; however, there is an organizational framework that will allow for purposeful instruction and independent practice: literacy workshops.

Literacy workshops offer students a variety of practical benefits. They enable students to practise skills that they have already been effectively taught and to consolidate learning. They promote collaboration and student interdependence; they also foster learner engagement and independent practice of learning in diverse contexts (although, of course, careful and responsive planning and negotiation are needed).

Although every classroom has its own culture with a set of rituals, routines, and expectations, it is important to meet the following criteria for instructional practices and individual activities in all literacy workshops:

- explicit linking to other parts of the class or classroom culture (Instructional practices and individual activities are not stand-alone, isolated events.)
- explicit statement of the learning purposes for an activity (There is no guesswork for students.)
- the promotion of engagement in social interaction and cognitive collaboration (Students must, therefore, be taught strategies for productive and accountable talk.)
- encouragement for students to integrate and transfer meaning across the language arts, multiple intelligences, and literacies
- a range of responses considered acceptable, with emphasis on there not being just one right answer
- developmental appropriateness (Cambourne, 2001)

We will then be able to maximize success.

The overall goal of literacy workshops is to generate *navigators*: students and teachers who can plan, direct, and travel their routes towards literacy; who make use of multiple tools and texts to read their environment, chart their course, and make adjustments when necessary. As navigators of literacy, students and teachers can smoothly blend theory and practice, reception and expression of information through the language arts, and thinking, doing, and becoming.

Essential Elements of Literacy Workshops

Workshops rely heavily on the organizational structures of literary warm-ups, mini-lessons, anchor charts, literacy notebooks, individual conferences, and literacy centres.

Literary warm-ups

Literary warm-ups, which take about five minutes, can feature read-alouds, encounters with texts of many different types, quick activities that activate prior knowledge, or book talks by students or teacher. They might also contain highlights of previous workshops and brief student presentations or responses. They are designed to energize and motivate students, to prepare them for productive and accountable work. The goal should be to learn in a joyful, active, and engaging way.

For example, to introduce the genre of nonsense verse or maybe fantasy, engage the class in a whole-group choral reading of "Hey, Diddle, Diddle." Because nursery rhymes are often familiar to students, they are effective texts to use as hooks, or warm-ups; they are also easily accessible as public domain texts. To make the choral reading more interesting, experiment with voices (e.g., a big bear voice, a tiny mouse voice); dynamics (e.g., reading loudly or in a whisper), and emphasis. Have parts of the class read alternate lines. Elicit suggestions about how the rhyme can be read aloud.

Mini-lessons and anchor chart use

Mini-lessons are teacher-initiated, whole-group instructional sessions for constructing, extending, and revising meaning. They typically take 5 to 10 minutes. The teacher generally derives topics for mini-lessons from the assessment and observation of what students need to know on a particular day so that they will be able to read, write, and navigate texts better tomorrow. The teacher selects strategies that will prepare students to read, write, and navigate new texts successfully and independently, or support them in their continued development. Mini-lessons may be procedural (where the teacher responds to issues of "how-to"), but flexibility is also important. Teachers may use a combination of modelled, shared, or interactive writing or reading, or they may use published works, often touchstone texts, as models or *mentor texts* to demonstrate the focus of the mini-lesson.

In your first workshop mini-lessons, focus on workshop components and what the students need to know to be successful (e.g., routines and expectations; management of time, space, and resources; self-monitoring, self-assessment, and goal setting in the workshop; selection, management, and organization of reading, writing, and literacy work).

Mini-lessons are often accompanied by the creation of anchor charts, which are made accessible to students during the workshop. Here is how an anchor chart might develop:

Gather students and explain that today the class will establish expectations and procedures for the literacy workshop. Brainstorm with students a list of conditions that would allow them to be successful in the workshop. Students might say having a quiet space to work, knowing what to do and how to act in the workshop, knowing where to find resources and how to store their work, and understanding what to do if they get stuck. Through shared writing, record all responses on chart paper or use an interactive whiteboard. Provide solutions and procedures as you write. For example, if students ask about sharpening pencils, remind them of the Sharp Tip routine.

Invite and challenge students to consider all these guidelines when they are engaging in literacy work during the workshop. Encourage them to add to the list

Mentor Texts
Extending the concept of touchstone texts, *mentor texts* are published texts that offer teachers and students opportunities to learn from authors' ideas, structures, or written craft. As students gain comfort with mentor texts through read-alouds and mini-lessons, they begin to read like writers, applying ideas, structures, or techniques of the craft to their own writing.

Sharp Tip
To keep work flowing in an uninterrupted, quieter setting, sharpen pencils ahead of time! Keep two labelled jars for pencils, one for sharp and one for dull. When students need a sharpened pencil, they simply exchange their old pencil for a fresh one.

if they realize something is missing. At the end of the day's workshop, review the chart with students, confirming, clarifying, and extending as necessary. Review the chart again at the beginning of the workshop for the next few days, encouraging students to talk about what is working well, what needs clarification, and what should be added or removed. Once you feel that procedures are well established, create and post an anchor chart for ongoing reference.

We recommend use of anchor charts that meet the following five criteria.

1. *Anchor charts have a single focus.* Ideas include guidelines for effective talk; what strategic readers or effective writers do; and ways to work independently in the literacy workshop.

2. *Anchor charts are co-constructed with students through shared writing.* The draft chart is left on a chart stand or interactive whiteboard, and students are encouraged to revise, clarify, and test it before final copy. This invitation builds student ownership and improves the likelihood that students will make meaningful and authentic use of a chart as a reference.

3. *Anchor charts have organized and consistent appearances.* They are easy to use — a consistent appearance or setup frees students to focus on the content.

4. *Anchor charts match the learners' thinking, the language used in the classroom, and the texts the learners have encountered.* They are written at students' instructional level.

5. *Anchor charts support ongoing learning.* Charts contain references to ongoing strategy use and skill development as opposed to records of how to do something specific.

Here is a model anchor chart.

Expectations for the Literacy Workshop

- If you're stuck, ask a peer to help, use the classroom resources, or change tasks.

- Share resources. Centre activities are cooperative.

- Keep all your work in your literacy notebook or folder. Keep everything! You never know when you might use it.

- Use an indoor voice. Respect the right of others to work quietly.

The core of the literacy workshop

Imagine a literacy workshop . . . a place where teachers and students are engaged both independently and collaboratively in an atmosphere of focused production. The teacher is working with a small group of students who are whisper-reading, seated in a way that allows full sight of the room; running records are being conducted. Another group of students are actively discussing the text that they have just finished reading. The students are planning how to respond and share their text with the rest of the class. At the computer centre, students are reading content texts with text-to-speech technology; they are gathering information for their upcoming inquiry project. Tucked in the back corner is a small group that is quietly preparing a readers theatre script to perform during Sharing Time. Yet one more group is actively engaged with the literacy lead teacher who has joined the class to reinforce specific literacy strategies. The remaining students (either alone or with a partner) are working in different places in the classroom; their literacy notebooks are open as they gather words, thoughts, and ideas for the stories and poems they've decided to work on. Each group has placed itself close to the anchor charts that serve as tools for the day's literacy work.

Independent student learning and practice are at the core of the literacy workshop. Students may take part in one or more activities based on their needs and goals established during mini-lessons and on the workshop structures in place in the classroom. At times, workshops have a specific focus where students are required to engage in assigned reading, writing, and literacy work (as in inquiry- and project-based workshops, described below). Length of time block (generally 60 to 75 minutes) may depend on grade level or be mandated by the school district.

Literacy workshops are often supported by literacy centres, small work areas in the classroom where students work independently or in small groups on tasks designed to practise what has been previously introduced in modelled, shared, and guided work. Groupings for literacy work should be flexible. They will vary dependent on the purpose of the task and the desired goal. Teachers sometimes intervene with just-in-time instruction for individuals or small groups as needed; at other times, they will work alongside students at literacy centres, engaging as participants or observers. While students are fully engaged in collaborative activities at literacy centres, teachers work with small groups (e.g., for guided reading or a specific focus in writing); they also circulate, provide support, and conduct conferences.

Literacy notebooks or portfolios

Literacy notebooks or portfolios are valuable ways of keeping track of learning; they also serve as a useful assessment tool to look at growth over time. Inside students' notebooks, we might find

Within a literacy notebook, the student can keep a day-by-day tracking sheet with two columns. The student writes comments and reflections on the left side and the teacher comments on the right side.

- learning goals, plans, and reflections on their process, journey, and destination
- snippets of words and texts, doodles, illustrations, and ideas gathered along the students' literacy journeys
- texts encountered or created in the classroom with initial reactions, notes, or ideas for responses
- texts that the students want to encounter or create at some point in their travels
- representative samples of work completed during mini-lessons, small-group lessons, or literacy centre activities
- literacy works in progress and literacy works that have reached their final destination
- samples of literacy works that capture student growth over time
- observations and feedback of travellers encountered along the way, including the teacher, peers, and family

Individual conferences

Hold conferences with each student as regularly as possible, for both reading and writing. You can initiate conferences with students, either based on a schedule or immediate observed needs. Observe and record, perhaps using a clipboard with class list or a posted "status of the class" list to identify and track individual and group needs. Student and teacher listen to one another or they read, react, reinforce strategies, ask questions, and evaluate progress towards old goals and set new ones. It is important for the teacher to establish rapport, share, listen, comment, encourage, and guide during these conferences. Conferences may include formal assessments, informal reading/writing inventories, and think-alouds.

If you are adopting a schedule, post it at the start of the week with spots for five students a day so that every student in the class has an assigned time; otherwise, you can post a schedule at the start of each workshop day, based on who needs or wants a conference that day. In this case, you would start the list and then invite students to sign up if they would like a conference that day.

Sharing Time

A large-group gathering, either formal or informal, is usually held at the conclusion of each workshop period. Student oriented, its primary purposes are for sharing, feedback, and response from an audience of peers. Students sign up in advance to share literacy work, which may be a completed piece or a work in progress in need of feedback. The emphasis should be on celebrating and on offering helpful suggestions for improvement. This time is the students' opportunity to share what they are working on or to highlight something interesting they've encountered during their literacy work.

Ways to Support Literacy Work in the Workshop

- During the first weeks of school, establish procedures for predictable, productive, and organized workshops with regular instruction based on the assessment of students' ongoing needs.
- Organize classroom space for large-group, small-group, and individual work. Arrange furniture to allow for easy flow between centres. If space is severely limited, keep task cards, materials, and resources in appropriately sized bins so that the students can transport them to their group tables (the bins often serve as mobile centres).
- Ensure that students know how to obtain and return resources (e.g., paper, notebooks, files, texts, and reference materials).
- Rather than imposing expectations, deadlines, and goals for the workshop, negotiate them.
- Ensure that routines at centres are modelled and clarified on a regular basis. (Use role play as a tool to model productive behavior.)
- Maintain literacy (reading and writing) portfolios and notebooks in a consistent place to permit easy access. Individual student folders organized by first names can be stored on mobile carts, thereby allowing students to retrieve them for each workshop, keep works-in-progress in a central location, and return them to the same location. The folders can then be used during conferences to discuss current work and for ongoing assessment.
- Co-construct anchor charts with students during mini-lessons and subsequent workshops in order to build student ownership. Post them as reference points for students.
- Ensure that students know how to solve problems when you are working with small groups.
- Designate "quiet days" to allow productive independent reading and writing time while some students are working at centres. On a designated quiet day, the activity at the centre is chosen from a list of low noise–level activities. Alter-

The Importance of Routines
"I spend the first two months on routines — where things go, how they are used, how we move from centre to centre, how we talk, write and read quietly, and so on. My goal is for students to become independent doers with full responsibility for classroom materials. Once the routines are established, I only have to open my mouth to teach."
— Susan Sitter, a teacher with Nipissing-Parry Sound Catholic District School Board

Finding a Time and Place for Everything
For an exemplary practical guide on how to organize your day and your classroom for literacy work, see the videos by Irene Fountas and Gay Su Pinnell: *Managing the Day* (Part 1) and *Planning for Effective Teaching* (Part 2). Grade 1 teacher Kate Roth — nicknamed "Kate the Great" by our teacher candidates — takes you through her classroom and her routines, where everything has a scheduled time and place, and where all materials are clearly labelled for student use and maintenance. This model is achievable — it works!

native task cards may be used. At the readers theatre centre, for example, the activity could be script writing and individual, silent rehearsal.

Maintaining smooth management

Establishing predictable routines and creating engaging learning activities can usually prevent management difficulties — usually, but not all the time. Your whole class may have settled happily into workshop routines by mid-October, but then a new entrant appears and upsets the pattern. One child may be having a bad day because she didn't get enough sleep. Another may have ongoing self-regulation difficulties. The following strategies work well for teachers:

- Create your working groups so that more independent students can support the less independent. Leaders can guide students not yet familiar with the routines. This approach promotes positive leadership and creates a healthy classroom community.
- Balance times for choice and times when you assign an activity. Be sure to rotate who gets to choose first and ensure that the children know when it will be their turn.
- Remove any child who is disrupting learning at a centre during workshop time.

Cunningham and Allington (2006, p. 218) offer these assurances:

> Eventually, if you are determined and persistent, your centers will work almost without you. Leaders will care for materials, and children will know which days they get to choose first. The occasional child who must be removed will, after sulking for a few minutes, write the required explanation so that he or she can go to centers the next day.

Inquiry- and Project-Based Literacy Workshops

"Critical inquiry focuses on larger systems of meaning and connects the personal with the political. Critical inquiry involves the active engagement of learners as they explore issues in the world around them. . . . Critical inquiry weaves critical literacy practices throughout the curriculum and offers children prolonged engagement with issues that are important to them and important to democracy. In such contexts, children read against texts, re-envision the world they live in, and take action within that world."
— Tasha Laman (2006, p. 204)

Inquiry- and project-based literacy workshops enable students to engage in critical inquiry, a key aspect of what they need to navigate life. They support students as they explore topics or content areas that have the potential to make a difference to them, their school, and beyond. Students are encouraged to explore through texts of many types problems that they have identified or found in their lives, in their classroom or school, in their community, or in the world beyond. A week is typically spent on a project of this nature.

It is important that students generate the topics. Their topics will be diverse, reflecting personal experience and what they feel has importance in their lives. Individual or partner topics may be related to greening and keeping the schoolyard clean, understanding community roles, and addressing bullying in the classroom.

Engaging students in inquiry- and project-based literacy workshops extends their literacy work to the community and helps them to make real-world connections. In essence, this type of inquiry allows students to look closely at their lives in an effort to make the world a better place. Students begin to see that learning enables them to function in the world and can be of benefit not only to themselves but to others.

Preparing for the workshop

- Ensure that students have the prerequisite knowledge to identify ongoing issues. Construction of knowledge, initial investigation, and exploration can be provided through a variety of teacher-directed activities. These include direct teaching, field trips, guest speaker sessions, use of many types of texts, research, and class discussions.

- Brainstorm several issues that are related to your current theme or big idea and that require investigation, exploration, and social action. For example, as part of an ongoing exploration, students and teacher might brainstorm possible messages about environmental awareness and ways to share the messages with the larger community. Ensure that you draw clear links to the meaning and relevance in students' lives: remind students that they must care for the earth if they expect it to sustain them.

- Brainstorm with students additional references needed and where they can find them; take a trip to the school or community library if required; identify useful, reputable websites to use (see lesson plan in Chapter 4).

- Review various books, games, videos, and presentations — in other words, texts of many types — and emphasize that students have many different and creative ways of presenting their information.

- Brainstorm a list of possible projects or outcomes from the inquiry that will allow students to share their learning with others.

    Possible projects might include, but are not limited to a message-oriented picture book; an A B C book; a game; a model that demonstrates the issue and ways to resolve it; a media presentation; a video/documentary; or a speech or a letter to share with stakeholders.

- Brainstorm a list of audiences with students, perhaps other research groups, the class as a whole, parents, science or heritage fair participants and judges, or younger students.

- Ensure that students have decided on the type of project they will be producing and that they have gathered all necessary resources. Encourage students to bring in materials from home and to prepare lists of required materials that can be gathered in the school (e.g., colored paper, art materials, game cards, Bristol board, and clay).

Daily workshop setup

This setup is based on a weeklong workshop with independent student work at its core.

Before independent literacy work

- Conduct mini-lessons, as required. Some days you might be giving one; other days you might conduct three mini-lessons with three different groups. Mini-lessons at the beginning of the week tend to focus on planning; towards the end of the week, the focus may be more on presentation and sharing. You may use a mentor text as a guide for how to organize an informational text (e.g., *Diary of a Worm* by Doreen Cronin), demonstrate the structure and key characteristics of a game (e.g., Trivial Pursuit), or for a digital presentation, review characteristics of various effective websites (e.g., *National Geographic*) and accompanying media presentations. During mini-lessons, explore with students how the author or designer uses special features to communicate information and how text features, such as titles, headings, color, glossary, index, photographs/illustrations, and animation are used.

- Connect each mini-lesson focus to project work by discussing with students how similar text features and organizational structures might be used as enhancements.
- Remind students of workshop expectations: these will have been posted in the classroom since the beginning of the school year. Ensure that they know where to find and store resources and materials required.

During independent literacy work
- Allow students to work independently, either alone or with a partner, gathering information and preparing their project.
- Monitor learning and intervene with guided reading/writing groups or conferences as needed, offering lessons on fiction reading strategies or organizing information using expository text structures and graphic organizers; on interpreting information conveyed in tables of contents, indexes, glossaries, sidebars, illustrations, pictures, diagrams, graphs, and maps; and on how to analyze, critique, compare, assess, and evaluate to reduce the likelihood of plagiarism.

After independent literacy work
- Sharing Time focuses on discussing the content area and evaluating student understanding, beginning with questions such as "What did you think? What did you learn?" Encourage students to share reactions and to ask questions to clarify; decide whether reading goals have been achieved; check whether questions have been answered; seek more information from other sources (if required); share status of projects with the class and seek feedback.

Beyond today's independent literacy work into tomorrow
- Provide ongoing strategy instruction and modelling to improve content-area reading through a range of teaching strategies and approaches (e.g., mini-lessons and conferencing).
- Provide multiple opportunities for students to explore content-area reading and writing that allow them to internalize content.
- Return to exemplary mentor texts; discuss text features. Ask, "How can you make use of similar features in your presentations?" Encourage students to comment on next steps for their own projects, incorporating feedback on an ongoing basis.

Workshop Products as Something to Share: Mike Parr

Identifying several central issues worthy of further exploration and investigation without rigidly defining *how* to achieve the objectives gives students a sense of ownership over the direction their learning will take. Once the expectation for what is to be explored and learned is set, appropriate tasks or samples of types of appropriate learning activities should be explored. The teacher's role is to ensure that all students come to see that they have an active part in determining exactly what their learning activities, and their role in constructing these activities, will be. Teachers should challenge students to be creative — collectively where needed — and to demonstrate that they are able to develop a product that is worthwhile and has purpose.

Sharing activities and products that reflect student learning can be done in the class, with other classes throughout the school, in other classes throughout the board, and even in the wider community. When students share their work and see the learning and excitement that their work can generate, they see purpose! Such opportunities allow even reluctant learners to stand back and reflect with pride on the fact that they have shared something of themselves that is good and benefits others. It's difficult to find greater purpose than that.

Mike is now an associate professor in the Schulich School of Education at Nipissing University.

Setting Up Centres Within the Literacy Workshop

Literacy centres, or areas organized for independent and small-group literacy work, enable us to respond to the interests of all students, differentiate instruction in multiple ways, keep the learning child centred and social based, and teach within students' comfort zones. Students are given legitimate choices and opportunities to work at their own rate. Groupings are typically heterogeneous, ranging from 2 to 4 students. They thus allow for collaboration and minimize unproductive behavior; they can be either teacher or student selected, dependent upon the group and the task.

Literacy centre procedures

1. Before centre work gets under way for the day, review expectations for behavior and task completion. Depending on your system, let students know how you will signal the end of work at one centre or rotation to the next. As they move to their first centre, ensure that they all know where they are going and with whom they will be working. Introduce any new centres or alterations to centres through modelling or demonstration; read through the centre task card and answer student questions. For example, before setting up a Meet the Masters centre, described below, you will want to model how to find, use, and store art supplies.

2. During centre work, you will need to have three systems at work.

   First, you need a system that allows you to determine where students are — management boards, where each student has a name card that is inserted into one of the centre's pockets, work well. There is one pocket per student allowed at the centre. Centres can be student selected or teacher assigned. With such a system, you can quickly look up and see whether all students are where they are supposed to be.

   Second, you need a system that allows students to keep track of work they do at centres and which centres they have completed. Some teachers place an inbox at each centre that gathers work done each day; others maintain a workshop folder that contains all work produced during workshop and centre time.

   Third, since you will be working with small groups of students some of the time, you will need to have in place a system that allows students to contact you if — and only if — it is critical. We find it particularly useful to designate one student who can interrupt the teacher during work with small groups; all other students in the classroom ask questions of the designate, except under unusual or emergency circumstances, such as danger or blood!

Maximizing Time with a Small Group: Michelann Parr

When teaching Grade 1, I ensured that my groups were well balanced with regard to behavior and ability. To achieve this, I often took these two measures: (1) I drew my guided reading group from two or three other groups. (2) I selected a communicator for each literacy workshop block — a student who could write independently and solve problems well. I could typically identify five eligible students in each class. These students were provided with sticky notes and if there was a problem that they couldn't solve, they would write it down and slide it to me while I was working with my small group. I would, in turn, write a response, or wait until I could take a break to respond to the question. The only exception to this rule was if an emergency arose. (I would previously have brainstormed a list of what constituted an emergency with the students.)

3. After centre work, plan Sharing Time to allow students to reflect on their learning for the day and ask questions that would help them to extend their learning. Prompt them to reflect on what they did, what went well, what they learned, and what they might try tomorrow. Sometimes these questions will be general; at other times, they will be more specific and related to specific themes or centres in the classroom (e.g., the Meet the Masters centre, described on pages 36 to 37). This time is a prime opportunity to determine what you need to clarify before your next centre rotation.

At the end of each week, you might ask students to share their favorite task or greatest learning for the week.

Types of literacy centres

Many teachers use a combination of permanent and temporary literacy centres. Permanent centres are in place all year long. Many primary classrooms have the following: reading, writing, word solving, computer, poetry, listening, read-the-room, and journalling. At the read-the-room centre, for example, students choose a pointer and move about the room reading texts that are on display. They might also gather words of a specific pattern as they are reading. During Sharing Time, they might read aloud their favorite text. What might change is the theme or content of each centre. Temporary centres serve a specific purpose, often extending the learning that is taking place in the classroom; they are often dismantled once the task is complete, for example, following written instructions to make an anatomically correct insect from recycled and found materials.

Tasks at centres can be tiered in terms of complexity, thereby allowing for heterogeneous groups. At a word study centre, for example, students could choose between spelling the words using magnetic letters, writing the words out, stamping the words, making the words with playdough, drawing pictures to accompany words, or writing sentences with the words (Arquette, 2006). There can be differentiated instruction within one centre.

Sample centre task cards

Independent use of literacy centres can be facilitated through task cards that document the materials needed as well as outline procedures; usually one task card per centre is sufficient. Many teachers ensure that all task cards follow a similar format and are written at the instructional level of most of their students. Ensure that the text is clear and readable. While students enjoy clip art, graphics, borders, and color, such enhancements should be used sparingly in a way that does not detract from the task. For younger students, a pictorial list and set of procedures work well (see listening centre below). At times, task cards are supported with a model or exemplar of the task to be accomplished. Students who are taught how to use task cards through mini-lessons and shared reading are far less likely to require support at centres. Here are samples of teacher-created task cards that students have used to pursue centre work without direct teacher involvement.

Listening task card (Primary)

Can you hear what I hear?

As a group, listen to the story on CD, and follow along.

As a group, listen to the story on CD, and read along.

As a group, turn off the CD, and read together.

Turn to a partner, and read the story.

As a group, listen to the story on CD again.

Turn to a partner, and talk about your reading.

Be ready to share your story with the class.

Procedural writing task card (Junior)

PROCEDURAL – HOW DO!

1. **ON YOUR OWN**, read the recipes, game directions, activity instructions, and task cards provided at the centre.
2. What do you notice about the directions?
3. Choose an activity that you would like to teach to someone else.
4. Choose a format (e.g., recipe, game directions, activity instructions, task cards).
5. Assume that the person you will be teaching has never done your activity before. Write out your directions step-by-step in a way that they can read your directions and do the activity independently.
6. **WITH A PARTNER**, swap your instructions. Can your partner follow them easily? Are there any missing steps?
7. **ON YOUR OWN**, revise, edit, and write a polished copy.

MATERIALS:
A selection of recipes, game directions, science investigations, and art projects
Paper, pencils

Creating a Literacy-Enriched Play Centre

"Play is the highest expression of human development in childhood, for it alone is the free expression of what is in a child's soul."
— Friedrich Froebel

"Because children's uses of language in play reflect uses in the real world, play helps them develop sociocultural discourses." (Owocki, 2001, pp. 157–158)

Literacy-enriched play centres allow children to expand their knowledge of the world and written language through play. By using print within the context of play, children begin to understand not only how written language is used but to appreciate its many features (e.g., letters, letter–sound relationships, spelling, meaning, and punctuation) (Owocki, 2001).

While many play centres can be literacy enriched (e.g., the house centre, the construction centre, the hospital centre), one of our favorites is Meet the Masters. This centre is designed as a play area that extends a shared classroom experience, in this case, a trip to an art gallery. It is set up as an art gallery with room not only to create but also to display, view, and discuss art. It allows students to be in role as an artist, visitor, or gallery worker. Familiar reading, writing, and artistic materials are provided for students to explore and use.

This centre involves providing a classroom space where art can be worked on over time and its progress towards completion discussed. The teacher can engage students in talking about art on an ongoing basis, discussing such proverbs as "Beauty is in the eye of the beholder" or "One person's junk is another's treasure."

Using books such as *Beautiful Oops!* by Barney Saltzberg, it is possible to teach students that in art, they never need to worry about making a mistake — they can change what they are doing or repeat it — make it look like the final product was always meant to be. Many children are impressed to discover how much time professional artists need to complete a painting or sculpture.

A detailed outline of how to implement this centre, which provides many opportunities for critical thinking, follows.

Brainstorm and wonder

Brainstorm what students already know about art galleries. Ask: "Who works in an art gallery or frame shop? Who arranges the displays? What materials do they use? What is the purpose of an art gallery?" In so doing, you are allowing them to explore roles and perspectives, to see the familiar in a fresh, critical way.

Generate other questions with students, too — things they wonder about or want to know. Some samples: Who cleans the gallery? Who decides what art is displayed? Who writes the brochures and advertisements? How many tries or practices does an artist have before it is finished? What do artists do with the work they don't like?

Build background knowledge

- Tour an art gallery, studio, museum, or framing shop. Prepare the students carefully by providing specific things to look for, do, and ask.
- Invite an artist, an art gallery director, or a museum docent to do a show and tell followed by a question-and-answer period.
- Share children's books on art and artists (e.g., *The Art Lesson* by Tomie dePaola, *It Looked Like Spilt Milk* by Charles G. Shaw, *The Magic Paintbrush* by Robin Muller, *Beautiful Oops!* by Barney Saltzberg, *The Dot* and *Ish* by Peter Reynolds, and *The Artist* by John Bianchi).
- Select masters of art (e.g., Picasso, Mondrian, van Gogh, and Monet) and elements of art (e.g., line, color, texture), and ensure that models are displayed, viewed, and discussed. Elicit suggestions from students as well. (These may be artists that they have seen highlighted in books or on TV shows; for example, students might suggest trying out the Jackson Pollock–type of painting that they saw in *Olivia* by Ian Falconer.)

Structure the environment

Centre Materials
paper of different sizes, colors, textures, and gloss
crayons, pastels, pens, paints, pencils
clay, mixed media
glue, tape
cardboard, mat boards, and Bristol board for framing
permanent markers for making tickets, gallery maps, and brochures
index cards for art labels (name of artist, title of work, brief description)

To create a gallery in the classroom, rope off a corner so there is space to hang children's art, a shelf for sculptures, a ticket stand where visitors can buy tickets and pick up brochures (produced by the children or from a real gallery), an easel, and tables for sculpting and framing.

Owocki's *Make Way for Literacy* discusses this kind of centre in detail (2001, pp. 164–167).

Extending Your Literacy Centre Repertoire

Permanent literacy centres typically include reading, computer, interest, and poetry. Once established, they run themselves; when relevant, only the content needs to change. Extending your repertoire does not necessarily mean implementing new centres; instead, you can tweak or rethink what you ask students to do at permanent centres.

Expand use of your computer centre. Bookmark two or three excellent websites for research on a specific topic, perhaps researching an author, discovering the history of a nursery rhyme, or learning about the solar system. Alternatively, teach students how to use Comic Life, PowerPoint, Keynote, or iMovie to create colorful media presentations to demonstrate their learning. ("Creating Digital Stories Together" in Chapter 10 outlines how one teacher approached the technology challenge.)

Transform the reading centre into a Meet the Author centre. Allow children to design ways of presenting favorite authors, their works, and their life stories. This centre can be used to highlight community authors, family members, and students' own works.

Create interest centres that are responsive to what students want to know. Designate one centre to reflect a current interest, for example, weather. A weather station centre could include taped weather reports for TV or radio, sample newspaper reports, and a bookmarked website dedicated to weather. At other times, the interest centre can become something else, such as a school office, a veterinarian's office, or a space station.

Keeping Track of Learning in Literacy Workshops

Tools for Tracking

Plan to use a variety of the following:
• checklists
• tracking sheets
• rubrics
• work samples
• success criteria

Assessment in literacy workshops can take a variety of formal and informal formats, but each should reflect the individual goals set by the students, the teacher, and curricular expectations. Through conferencing, observation, and analysis, reader and writer behaviors can be assessed. Assessment practices should be designed to provide constructive feedback and facilitate learning.

Engagement is an essential characteristic of literacy workshops, so part of the responsibility for assessment should be shared with the students, especially as they evaluate their growth as readers, writers, and navigators and their progress towards set goals. Teachers share the assessment process with students as they conference and examine reading responses, journals, and a variety of writing samples.

For independent work throughout the workshop, it is a good idea to design tracking sheets and self-assessment checklists. Students can thereby monitor their own progress and record their centre and task choices. For younger students, pictorial tracking sheets are used: these weeklong sheets typically ask students to note where they went and to reflect on whether they felt happy, indifferent, or disappointed about their literacy centre work. Teachers can then debrief orally with students.

With older students, tracking sheets may also include sections for student self-assessment and teacher comments. These can be specific to a centre, a workshop, or a longer time.

Use of a junior tracking sheet such as this one promotes organization and self-monitoring.

Tracking Sheet for Inquiry- or Project-Based Workshop

☐ I have decided whether I am working alone or with a partner.

☐ I have decided how I am going to present my information (e.g., picture book, media presentation, game).

☐ I have gathered informational texts and resources related to my topic.

☐ I have selected graphic organizers and/or expository text structures to organize my information.

☐ I have developed a timeline of activities.

☐ I have collected materials that I expect to use to prepare my project.

More detailed assessment practices that can take place in literacy workshops will be presented in subsequent chapters.

> **Literacy Essential 3:** A workshop structure with warm-ups, mini-lessons, independent study, centre activities, and conferences combines theory and practice and enables students and teachers to develop independently and collaboratively as navigators of literacy.

In Touch with Families

Highlight the learning that takes place in the classroom through weekly newsletters that can include anchor charts for implementation at home. For example, a chart might address "What do I do when I get to a word that I don't know?" It can be co-created with students. As the year progresses, students may be able to assume the roles of newsletter writer and editor.

Invite parents, grandparents, and caregivers to spend an hour taking part in a segment of a day with their children. For example, they could spend the first hour of the morning seeing how routines and a read-aloud are conducted. Ask visitors to record briefly three things they noticed in the classroom that they can try at home.

CHAPTER 4

Constructive, Accountable Talk

Oral language is the foundation of literacy development: there is a common base serving all three activities of talking, reading, and writing
— Marie Clay (2004)

Talk is an umbrella term that covers the wide range of activities involved in listening, speaking, conversing, discussing, and engaging in dialogue, from the informal clamor on the playground to more formal *grand conversations*, or the structured dialogues of a literature circle discussion. Talk is a vital medium through which learning of all kinds occurs. In many cases, talking and listening make learning possible.

Recognizing the Value of Talk

"Children need multiple opportunities to talk about text in order to appropriate the connections between spoken and written representations of meaning.... What they need from school is a continuation of the same sort of meaningful engagements in reading and writing [that they may have had at home] with responsive assistance when they are unable to complete a task on their own."
— Gordon Wells (2003, pp. 10–11)

Talk as described above is essential in language development. Lively classrooms include time for playful speaking and listening activities, such as poetry and drama games. There are also appropriate times for constructive, accountable talk. The term *accountable talk* refers to talk that is meaningful, respectful, and mutually beneficial to both speaker and listener (Allen, 2002). Strategies for talk of all kinds will be introduced in this chapter and will be an ongoing topic in the rest of the book.

There are powerful interconnections between the development of oral language and literacy. The fact that oral language is learned in use, in a variety of real-life contexts, and under identifiable learning conditions, informs our teaching of literacy. We also know that the same neural machinery used for oral language is used in literacy activities. It therefore makes sense to promote growth in listening and speaking skills in the classroom literacy program from the early years and beyond to build the necessary foundations for literacy learning.

Brian Cambourne (2000/2001) identifies these key conditions for learning how to talk and for becoming literate:

- *immersion* in resources and opportunities for practice (lots of talk, plenty of texts)
- *demonstration* or expert modelling of the ability (talking or reading) to be acquired
- *expectations* on the part of those with whom the learner is bonded that the learner will achieve or succeed (these expectations are understood implicitly in the early years and should be explicitly discussed in formal contexts)

- *responsibility* for decision-making on the part of the learners about what, when, and how to learn
- *responses* consisting of relevant, timely, and appropriate feedback from knowledgeable others
- *employment or use* of the time and opportunity to practise what is being learned in functional, authentic ways (Diverse groupings — for example, whole group, partner, and triad — are essential here in order to maximize student participation.)
- *approximations* or the freedom to make mistakes as the desired model is approached
- *engagement* as the key condition throughout all of the above conditions and the guiding principle when choosing effective oral language strategies

For more detail, see our earlier book, *Teaching the Language Arts: Engaging Literacy Practices*, especially pages 42–43, 107–8.

Emergent and struggling speakers, readers, and writers, including English Language Learners, require the use of explicit instruction and effective strategies to enhance oral language. They also require diverse opportunities to talk and be listened to, and multiple opportunities for feedback and response. Cambourne's model is critical in the development of oral language, particularly with those who are learning English as a second language or for those whose oral language development requires a little more time and practice.

Talk should be maximized and planned for throughout the classroom curriculum. Transition minutes (e.g., before recess, after the bell, waiting for morning announcements) can be sponged up with effective oral language activities. Here are two examples.

- *Primary — Oral Fill in the Blank.* With the whole class, start off a two-line rhyme, leaving the final word blank: How absurd! It looks like a _____ (bird); The story's been read; it's now time for _____ (bed). After several examples, the students can compose their own. This five-minute activity is great for focused listening and for developing phonemic awareness.

Sample Debate Topics
Soccer is a better game than hockey.
Recess is a waste of time.
Winter is more beautiful than summer.

- *Junior — Two-Minute Debate.* Assign the whole class a topic, and have students debate with a partner. Give each partner one minute: one to argue in favor, the other to oppose. You may want to post a sentence starter such as "You may be right, but I have a different idea . . ."

Listening to What Is Said

First of all, you need something that is worth talking about: it might be a thought-provoking picture book or novel, a news story, a controversial film, website, a poster, or a TV advertisement. Having several copies of the text or projected images is helpful.

Pre-teach or review routines for small-group discussion and drama activities, for example, how to start and stop on cue, how to use a "drama" voice without shouting, how to make sure everyone gets a turn. Please see anchor chart "Guidelines for Good Talk" (page 47). Present your chosen text with an explicit emphasis on *listening*.

Lesson Plan 1 on Oral Language
Selected Text: *Tough Boris* by Mem Fox
Tough Boris, it seems, is a stereotypical pirate. In this simply patterned illustrated text, he is described by a young cabin boy as tough, massive, and scary . . . until his parrot dies. The book is great to use for shared reading as well as to discuss the use of adjectives in writing.

> ### A Pattern to Be Broken: Terry Campbell
>
> Whenever I use this book [*Tough Boris*] as a read-aloud with teacher candidates, I recall the first time I read it to a Grade 3 class. The pattern, with one line on each illustrated page, goes like this: "Boris was tough. All pirates are tough. He was massive. All pirates are massive . . ." Children quickly join in the repeated "All pirates are . . .," which goes on for several pages. Then the pattern abruptly changes with "But when his parrot died . . ." and one young boy with a piercing voice inserted, "All parrots die!" (The next page actually says, "He cried and cried.")
>
> I took this as a reminder of the need for flexibility. I had originally planned a serious discussion about how it's okay to cry, whether you are a boy or a girl, a teacher, or a pirate. But the spell of the solemn message was now broken. Of course, we all laughed, so we discussed the author's use of humor instead.
>
> I think Mem Fox would approve.

Preparing students for listening and joining in

This plan can be used as a template for similar lessons at junior-grade levels: *The Naked Lady* by Ian Wallace would be an appropriate text.

Show and discuss the cover of *Tough Boris*. Ask: "What does it mean to be tough? What makes a pirate tough?" Talk to students about the pattern in the book and model using a different adjective. For example, you might say: "When I read, 'He was horrid,' you respond, 'All pirates are horrid.'"

Reading aloud

Read aloud *Tough Boris*. Expect and prompt student participation at sentences similar to the one modelled.

Debriefing and revisiting the text to understand character and author

After the first reading, ask questions, first for free responses: "What do you think? How do you feel?" Discuss the characters. Ask: "Who is telling the story? How do the illustrations tell us that? Who is Boris? Is he the main character? How do we know?"

Prompt students to pay attention to how Boris acts and feels during the story; guide them by turning to the relevant pages. Ask them whether they think the illustrations are consistent with the way Boris is described in the text.

After a second reading, encourage students to offer opinions on why Mem Fox wrote *Tough Boris*. Here's one:

> I think she wrote the book to show that even big tough pirates cry and that sometimes it's okay for boys to cry too.

Using Mem Fox's website, verify students' opinions and point out that one of her purposes for writing the book was to show boys it's okay to cry and to talk about crying.

Modelling use of discussion structures or conversation starters

Introduce and post discussion models (shown in bold) by relating them to the text read aloud. For example:

- Making connections: "Tough Boris **reminds me of the time** when my cat died and I didn't want to cry in front of my brother."
- Giving evidence to back up opinions: "**When I heard (read) that** the pirate was tough, **I thought** he was going to be mean to the boy, **but then I really looked** at the picture of Boris, and he didn't look mean."
- Adding to what others say: "**When Lucie said** she thought the pirates were all bad, I didn't because they didn't look scary in the illustrations."
- Validating one another's thoughts: "**I agree with** James. When I listened to that part of the story, I thought the same thing and felt sorry for Boris."

> *Student 1:* Tough Boris reminds me of the time I fell out of the tree and was really hurt, but didn't want anyone to know. I got up quickly and said, "I'm okay."
>
> *Student 2:* Yes, I like to be tough in front of my friends, but when I get home, I often tell my family how much I'm really hurt.

Encouraging independent oral response and practice

Hot seating works well with any familiar folk or fairy tale. Nursery rhymes are excellent sources of minimal scripts.

- *Example 1:* **Hot seating.** One student is Boris while the rest of the class asks questions about the character's thoughts, feelings, and background; the one student answers in role. Guide the students by asking good questions of your own. Record other beyond-the-text questions to ask Boris, the boy, other pirates, or the parrot. You can then prompt students to work in partners or triads, taking turns asking and answering questions like these in role.

  Hey, Boris, is it true that all pirates are greedy?

  What are some of your favorite treasures? Where do you keep them hidden?

A: I'm sorry.
B: What?
A: I said I'm sorry.
B: Sorry's just a word.

- *Example 2:* **Minimal scripts.** Introduce brief four-line scripts on index cards, written for two characters. Larry Swartz's *The New Dramathemes* provides excellent examples; otherwise, write four-line scripts from student conversations or texts read in the classroom. Have 3 or 4 scripts prepared. Prompt students to say the lines in different ways (e.g., as written, sadly, as whispers, angrily, while laughing, while shaking hands, back-to-back, on the phone). Brainstorm for further ideas on how to say scripts. Post the list you develop for use by students. Next, have students divide into partners and write a four-line script such as the one at left. Bring students back to the large group to present and celebrate sample interviews and scripts. Guide students to self-assess using a checklist.

Boy: I'm sorry your parrot died.
Boris: Thanks. He was my best friend.
Boy: I can be your friend.
Boris: Thanks. I need a friend.

Comparing Websites Collaboratively

Lesson Plan 2 on Oral Language
Selected Texts: Two author websites, one whose titles are most suitable for primary students; the other, for junior students

We chose the websites of Jan Brett and Chris Van Allsburg.

Involve junior students in navigating media by having them compare two author websites. The work of one author should be at grade level and the other should be intended for younger audiences. Use key criteria to compare Chris Van Allsburg's author website with Jan Brett's, which is suitable for primary students. Provide some criteria to get the students started (see page 45), and then co-construct other criteria that reflect student interests and the unique features of author websites.

This activity can be set up for a computer lab session or as a learning centre in the classroom for partner or small-group work.

Preparing for effective talk

Encourage students to share what they already know about websites and to formulate questions they might have.

Show two author websites (e.g., those of Chris Van Allsburg and Jan Brett). Ask: "What do you know about these authors? What do you wonder about? What do you notice?" Introduce the websites much as you would a picture book. Have students consider questions like these: "What should we look for in an author's website? What makes a first-rate site? What enhances a site? What detracts?"

Introduce and discuss basic criteria for evaluating a website: (1) Purpose or main message of the site is clear and straightforward; (2) Information presented is clear and understandable; (3) Text and graphics are balanced in a way that enhances the site's message; (4) Artwork, graphics, and photos are appealing; (5) Users can find their way around easily; (6) The site offers a variety of up-to-date and credible resources; and (7) Content is free from bias (specific groups not targeted or ignored).

Ask: "How can we tailor these criteria to suit an author's website? Are there criteria we need to revise or add?" Work together to adapt the criteria as the class thinks necessary. Students may identify the following:

Enhancements: interactive features, videotaped interviews, sample author readings, student work, pictures

Detractions: pop-up advertisements or commercialism — companies trying to sell their products

Post the checklist that you and the class have co-constructed in response to the question about criteria.

Talking to form consensus

- *Partner Work:* Direct students to work in partners at a computer to apply evaluation criteria to two author websites. Encourage them to highlight relevant criteria and make notes that summarize findings. Circulate, guide, and observe.
- *Small-Group Work:* Set up small discussion groups; encourage students to discuss their findings, looking for where they agree and disagree, and where they can reach consensus. Have them determine two key findings per website, one good feature, and one not-so-good feature (four points in all). Circulate, guide, and observe.
- *Large Group:* Allow time for each group to present a brief report on two key findings per website; take notes or have the students post them.

Applying what has been learned through talk

Encourage students to contact a children's author with their questions, concerns, and appreciation.

Suggest that students consult and refer to checklist criteria when they are planning their own website. One good source of information appears in *A Guide to Effective Literacy Instruction, Grades 4 to 6:* Vol. 7, published by the Ontario Ministry of Education. See Lesson 7 (Media Creation): Creating a Website.

Practising "Good Talk"

Teach students how to have a good discussion. Aim for lively, respectful interactions. You can provide explicit instruction in how to engage in "good talk" through modelling and give time for practice in small groups followed by feedback.

- One strategy is to hold informal mock debates, where students in partners or triads practise respectfully disagreeing after the teacher has showed what this practice sounds and looks like. The teacher and a partner, using a script prepared by the teacher, can model listening attentively with eye contact and provide sample statement starters such as "Yes, but I have a different idea . . ." You may assign the same topic for all pairs to debate, for example: (1) Reading on an e-reader is better than reading a book; (2) Being a student is better than being a teacher. Sample practice script for Topic 2:

  Pro: Students get to play with their friends at school.

  Con: Yes, that's true, but teachers are the ones in charge . . .

- Another strategy is to use role-plays to practise each of the criteria in "Guidelines for Good Talk," next page. These practice sessions can be followed by presentations and debriefing with the whole class.
  1. Introduce the task to students at the end of a mini-lesson or at the end of a literature discussion or grand conversation.
  2. Set the purpose: to practise a few "good talk" guidelines, for example, listening attentively and responding with questions or comments that build on each other's ideas.
  3. Model one role-play.
  4. Have students role-play in small groups, working with anchor chart criteria.
  5. Debrief with the small groups.

State explicitly the focus and purpose of the talk activity. Use organizational aids to help focus and track discussion, for example, anchor charts, graphic organizers, and task cards for role-playing.

Teach students how to disagree using respectful language, to build on each other's ideas, and to encourage all their group members to participate. Brainstorm examples of appropriate ways to disagree, for example:

"I'm not sure I agree with . . ." "I see it a different way . . ."

"I respect your right to . . ." "I understand what you're saying, but . . ."

Do not tolerate inappropriate comments. Depending on the context and circumstances, identify the comment and address the problem with the individual, the discussion group, or the whole class. You might use the situation in future role-plays.

Teach students how to enter appropriately into free-flow discussions and conversations (see task card and sample conversation next page).

Model and teach appropriate voice volume for classroom talk. Establish and maintain a noise level that allows students to hear what others are saying. Use flexible seating arrangements, for example, with students in a circle: the space limitation encourages quieter talk because the talk is directed towards listeners who are physically close. Use pairs, triads, and small groups to increase student participation.

Review success criteria and self-assessment criteria. Co-construct a "Good Talk" anchor chart with students. Use your observations of the needs of your classroom community, and conduct a whole-group discussion, based on prepared questions, such as, "How do you know when someone is listening?"

Begin the chart yourself, and then record student ideas. It could be as simple as this:

> When I am listening, my eyes are looking at the speaker,
> my mouth is closed, and my hands are still.

Post the chart in the classroom. Invite students to contribute to the rules and to problem-solve solutions to classroom issues during subsequent discussions.

Guidelines for Good Talk

Speak politely and at medium volume. Say *please* and *thank you*, and use your classmates' names.
Listen attentively. Use eye contact, keep an open mind, and have an open heart.
Focus on the topic or purpose of the discussion.
Respond with questions or comments that build on each other's ideas.
Back up your opinions with good reasons or evidence from the text.
Share responsibility for the group: take turns, stay on topic, and be positive and encouraging.

Building on each other's ideas: Sample task-card text

Laminated index cards work well because they can be posted in a permanent centre or included in a portable centre, where resources are organized in a basket and brought to a group table. This sample text is addressed to the student.

1. Record the title of the text you are discussing in your notebook.
2. In a group of three or four, sit in a circle.
3. First person retells the beginning, one or two retell the middle, and last person retells the ending.
4. Take turns posing a question that does not have a yes/no answer or choose a main theme for discussion based on the text.
5. As each question or topic is offered, go around the circle, sharing an opinion about it and listening to one another's ideas.
6. After listening carefully, respond by building. Say, for example, "I was wondering about that, too . . ." or "I didn't notice that — what made that stand out for you?" or "I had another idea about . . ."

A model "Good Talk" session that illustrates building on ideas

As part of a unit on government, a group of Grade 5–6 students discussed *The Other Place* by Monica Hughes, a novel that deals with a family moved to a penal colony in a not-so-distant future. The group tried to understand what some of the less common phrases meant and how this connected to what they had been learning about government. The children were heard saying this:

> *Eric:* What does this mean? [referring to *crimes of subversion*]
> *Taylor:* When you're spreading messages and you're trying to get into someone's head, without actually telling them what you are doing.
> *John:* Oh, like a newspaper. Oh, I think that's why he's going to prison. Because of the articles he wrote . . . I wonder what they said.

Eric: What's a penal colony? Oh, I think it's like a prison. Why would they say, "Long live the world government organization?" Does that mean that one government rules the world? That's like democracy. This is getting more interesting! I think I know what he is trying to do. He wants the world to have more than one government so he makes up lies about the world government, but are they true?

Tools and Contexts for Assessing Talk

Due to its very nature, talk is assessed in multiple contexts. You may find yourself listening in on informal recess conversations or literacy centre work. You may formally assess through individual or small-group conferences. You might look for something specific during small-group practice to see how students spontaneously use language or respond to others, or you might assess after students have had time to practise and explore specific oral language structures.

Regardless of when you assess, the purpose is to find out where students are at in their oral language so that you have a starting point for instruction in the classroom. Success criteria should be co-constructed with the whole group and posted on an anchor chart in the classroom. Here are sample criteria:

Success Criteria for Group Discussions or Grand Conversations

☐ I contributed my fair share to the discussion. (not too much, not too little)

☐ I was prepared for the discussion. (I read the text, had questions ready, and brought all needed materials.)

☐ I expressed my ideas clearly and supported them with reasons and evidence from the text.

☐ I made comments or asked questions to ensure that I understood other student's ideas.

☐ I thought about and extended other students' ideas in relevant ways.

☐ I made sure I understood any point of view I disagreed with and backed up my view with reasons.

☐ I helped keep the discussion on topic.

☐ I helped keep the discussion fair for everyone.

☐ I took part in the "group talk" after the discussion.

☐ I talked with the group about how to improve our discussions.

More Strategies for Promoting Constructive Talk

"Talk is like the sea . . . talk surrounds us and constitutes our primary mode of action. It is our medium, our atmosphere, and also our substance."
— D. L. Rubin (1990)

Depending on your circumstances and experience, you can either use the ideas below to extend your repertoire of strategies or to confirm strategies you already use to promote talking or listening,

Build add-a-sentence stories. Give a first sentence and then have each child add a sentence going around the circle, perhaps a small group of six or the whole class. This strategy can also be used to develop an account of a special event, school trip, or science experiment. The first sentence can be an evocative fictional setup, as in "She had warned them about opening the door, and now it was too late."

Engage students in "That reminds me of . . ." In this fast-paced activity, students recall favorite memories or stories. Once the teacher tells a quick story, for example, "I remember our first field trip last October, when we went to Science North on a bus . . . ," students jump in with their memories, beginning with the line "That reminds me of . . ."

Ask questions that call for positive answers. "Yes, I Can" is a fast-paced strategy during which a leader asks a question, such as, "Joanna, can you brush your hair?" and the student identified responds, "Yes, I can brush my hair," mimes the action, and then addresses another student with a new question.

Build listening skills, concept knowledge, and understanding of the language of instruction through barrier games, such as Battleship. Two students sit on either side of a screen or other physical barrier. They take turns giving instructions to each other to perform certain tasks — in other words, they take turns being speaker and listener. Instructions must be given clearly and followed carefully since the partners cannot see one another. Materials such as crayons, magnetic letters, shapes, and colored tokens can be used.

Engage students in participation stories, where they listen for specific words or sounds and add in sounds or phrases. Sharing the reading in this way makes the text more interesting. Students may also join in on sequential and recurring refrains or patterns — this activity is often referred to as *chiming in*. For example, children love chiming in on the chorus "terrible, horrible, no good, very bad day" as they listen to Judith Viorst's *Alexander and the Terrible, Horrible, No Good, Very Bad Day.*

Model the sharing of personal experiences through Show and Tell. Using a favorite photo, talk about who you are, where you came from, and what you like.

Tell stories using story element cards. In the story maker game, students draw one card from each of four piles: plot, setting, characters, and dialogue. In small groups, they begin telling a story based on their cards. To prepare, ensure that there are 4 to 6 color-coded cards in each category: each red card has a plot idea; each green, a setting; each yellow, a group of characters; and each blue, sample dialogue. Students may, when proficient with the game, contribute their own cards.

A home–school connection   **Promote oral language at home.** Parents, older peers, teachers, and other adults set a powerful example of good or poor communication. Communication skills are influenced by the examples children see and hear. Parents and teachers who listen to their children with interest, attention, and patience set a good example. Guidelines for developing children's oral language behavior (including specific suggestions for listening and speaking) can be distributed to families as suggestions. See page 52 for a sample page to send home.

Literacy Essential 4: Given the fact that talk is the foundation of literacy learning, promote accountable talk through explicit teaching and modelling, emphasizing that students interact with one another with respect, attentive listening, and an openness to new ideas.

Texts That Promote Talking and Listening

The following texts can be used as the basis for the lesson plans in this chapter. The emphasis is on ideas and issues worth listening to and talking about, from the humorous to the serious. These texts may also serve as mentor texts for oral language structures such as dialogue and as sources of vocabulary enrichment.

Illustrated fiction texts

The Top Secret Files of Mother Goose! by Gabby Gosling; illustrated by Tim Banks
Crow Boy by Taro Yashima
The Naked Lady by Ian Wallace
Old Turtle by Douglas Wood; illustrated by Cheng-Khee Chee
Rose Blanche by Roberto Innocenti
The Waiting Dog by Carolyn Beck; illustrated by Andrea Beck
The Wretched Stone by Chris Van Allsburg
Voices in the Park by Anthony Browne

Folk and fairy tales from around the world

The Three Little Pigs retold by James Marshall
Who's in Rabbit's House? A Masai tale retold by Verna Aardema
Talk, Talk: An Ashanti Legend retold by Deborah M. Newton Chocolate; illustrated by Dave Albers
The Legend of the Lady Slipper (Ojibwe tale) adapted by Lisa Lunge-Larsen and Margi Preus; illustrated by Andrea Arroyo

Texts on social issues

A Weekend with Wendell by Kevin Henkes
Willy the Wimp by Anthony Browne
17 Things I'm Not Allowed to Do Anymore by Jenny Offill; illustrated by Nancy Carpenter
Four Feet, Two Sandals by Karen Lynn Williams and Khadra Mohammad; illustrated by Doug Chayka
Bubba, the Cowboy Prince by Helen Ketteman; illustrated by James Warhola
All Those Secrets of the World by Jane Yolen; illustrated by Leslie Baker
Fanny's Dream by Caralyn Buehner; illustrated by Mark Buehner
Smoky Night by Eve Bunting; illustrated by David Diaz
Jack the Bear by Christina Leist
The Rabbits by John Marsden; illustrated by Shaun Tan
Christina Katerina and the Time She Quit the Family by Patricia Lee Gauch; illustrated by Elsie Primavera
What Really Matters Now . . . by Susan and Todd Montgomery

Illustrated information texts

Shin-chi's Canoe by Nicola I. Campbell; illustrated by Kim LaFave
Stellaluna by Janell Cannon
The Canadian Railroad Trilogy by Gordon Lightfoot; illustrated by Ian Wallace
Wolves by Tracy C. Read
Hana's Suitcase by Karen Levine

The Tree by Dana Lyons; illustrated by David Danioth

Chameleon, Chameleon by Joy Cowley; photographs by Nic Bishop

A Picture Book of Martin Luther King, Jr. by David A. Adler; illustrated by Robert Casilla

The Bus Ride That Changed History: Rosa Parks by Pamela Duncan Edwards; illustrated by Danny Shanahan

White Socks Only by Evelyn Coleman; illustrated by Tyrone Geter

Words Set Me Free: The Story of Young Frederick Douglass by Lesa Cline-Ransome; illustrated by James E. Ransome

Non-print media

Swimmy and More Classic Leo Lionni Stories (DVD Scholastic)

The Talespinners Collection (NFB of Canada)

Stellaluna (DVD)

Jeu (a wordless film about the chaos of modern life) (NFB of Canada)

Jumanji — Joe Johnstone's film adaptation of Chris Van Allsburg's illustrated book

Hana's Suitcase (CBC documentary)

Willy Wonka and the Chocolate Factory (adaptation of the Roald Dahl novel, Mel Stuart version)

Charlie and the Chocolate Factory (Tim Burton version)

Talking and Listening with Your Child

Talking is the first language art children use to express their own ideas and to further their own purposes. Recognize that you are a model for your child. Your child will listen to you and will try to repeat what you do and say. Be willing to follow your child's lead too. Talk about pictures and experiences, what's happening in a story, what your child did at school, or anything else your child finds interesting.

Suggestions for Developing Children's Language

- Chant nursery rhymes or sing simple action songs with repeated patterns, for example, "The Grand Old Duke of York," "Mary Had a Little Lamb," and "Row, Row, Row Your Boat." Visit the public library or even YouTube to find more examples.
- Help your child recognize and name colors, shapes, labels, numbers, and letters in the environment. For example, count the blocks as you stack them, and identify the color of each. Outside, discuss the graphics and colors of traffic signs.
- Encourage your child to share experiences and ideas by talking in short phrases or sentences. Some children need prompts or questions like this to get started: "What did you do at Nana's house?"

Guidelines for Modelling Good Listening Skills

- Be attentive. Children can tell whether they have your interest and attention by the way you do or do not reply. Maintain eye contact.
- Listen as patiently as possible. Children often take longer than adults to find the right word. Avoid cutting them off before they have finished speaking.
- Listen to nonverbal messages. Be attentive to tone of voice, facial expressions, energy level, and posture. You can often tell more from the way a child says something than from what the child has said.

Suggestions for Strengthening Listening Skills

It is a good idea to do the following activities with your child.
- Listen for and identify neighborhood sounds, perhaps the sounds of airplanes, trains, tractors, trucks, and children playing.
- Listen to the sounds of household appliances (e.g., blender, vacuum cleaner, washing machine, and stove timer).
- Listen for sounds outside, such as water running and wind blowing. Make this into a game. Say something like: "Shhhhh. Can you hear what I hear? I hear the wind blowing. What do you hear?"

Pembroke Publishers © 2012 *Balanced Literacy Essentials* by Michelann Parr, Terry Campbell. ISBN 978-1-55138-275-3

CHAPTER 5

The Modelling of Literate Behaviors

The benefits of being read to are many. First, from listening to stories read aloud, children become familiar with the cadences of written language and the generic structure of stories and other types of text. They also increase their vocabularies in domains that are rarely the subject of everyday talk. And, equally important, they learn that books are a source of interest and enjoyment that can introduce them to real as well as imaginary objects, places, and events that they do not encounter in their immediate environment.

— Gordon Wells (2003, p. 3)

As teachers, we recognize the power of reading aloud to children whether it's in the classroom or at home. We understand that a read-aloud is more than lifting words off a page for children, more than just a listening activity. Read-alouds open up opportunities for students to pay attention to texts of many types, experience the joy of reading, and want to be both readers and authors.

The role of reading aloud in a classroom program cannot be emphasized strongly enough. Research supports its key links to literacy, the love of reading, the development of concepts about print and text, and language development from the preschooler to the secondary student. An engaging read-aloud requires careful thought about what to read as well as how to read it.

Not every child is going to love every text, though. Some learners will prefer non-fiction and informational texts to stories and poems. Maximizing emotional and intellectual engagement of learners requires that you bring texts of many types, cultures, backgrounds, genres, and interests into your classroom. The task becomes one of balance and choosing the "just right" text for a given time. Achieving it requires that you have a range of texts to select from and the confidence to follow your own instincts about a particular text.

Choosing the "Just Right" Text for the Time

"The books that help you most are those which make you think the most. The hardest way of learning is that of easy reading; but a great book that comes from a great thinker is a ship of thought, deep freighted with truth and beauty."
— Theodore Parker

"Just right" texts appeal to learners on many levels. They may be delightful and entertaining or informative and enlightening. They are characterized by vivid language that makes the story or content come alive. They pose challenges — such as descriptive or technical vocabulary — which call for modelling and discussion. Fiction or literary texts to read aloud should be true-to-life and not too moralistic. They should address truths about life with sensitivity, regardless of possible controversy. Non-fiction and informational texts to read aloud should be relevant to learners, accurate, and factual. All texts selected for read-aloud offer many layers of meaning, multiple interpretations, conversation about perspectives and views taken by the author, and opportunities for engagement with aspects of the real world.

One foolproof method for determining whether a text is suitable for reading aloud is to read it out loud with the listener in mind. If the language flows fluently and lends itself to the creation of dramatic moments, then it will most likely work. Consider too whether the text is worth revisiting on multiple occasions, from multiple perspectives — perhaps it is a thought-provoking picture book or novel or a news story. Text type does not matter.

Texts we choose to read aloud are often different from those our students would select or they might be just beyond their independent reading level. In this way, we expose students to worlds, places, and cultures that they might not otherwise encounter on their own. Texts read aloud, regardless of whether they be newspaper articles, website content, picture books, novels, or poems, provide models of writing for students to explore, adapt, or borrow. For many students, reading aloud is a form of scaffolding that prepares them to read increasingly complex texts on their own. And for others, reading aloud frees them from the stress and pressure of reading independently and allows them access to higher-level thinking, instead of being limited to lower levels of word solving.

Ideally, teachers read aloud to students daily. As you do so, be sure to share with them your problem-solving strategies, decision-making processes, and guidelines for text selection. Did you choose the text because it models a particular grammatical structure or because the language is deliciously poetic? Did you choose the text because it presents content in an interesting way or because it is worth experiencing? Keep track of why you select particular books, and encourage your students to suggest texts that they think the whole class may enjoy.

What you may consider to be less than "just right" could be more than "just right" for students. When you choose books to read aloud, be sure to consider the needs, interests, and cultures of your students as well as curriculum demands. The anecdote below raises an interesting issue about choice.

The Bottom Line: Michelann Parr

Years ago, a teacher candidate returned from a placement with a copy of *The Waiting Dog* by Carolyn and Andrea Beck. My immediate response was, "How awful! Of course, I don't want to read it, let alone look at the pictures! What would possess (and I meant possess!) anyone to write a book that graphic, gory, and disturbing?"

Does the book have appeal? Absolutely. Is it informative? Yes, it is 100 percent anatomically correct right down to the *dirty thirty-twos* (referring to our teeth). Is the language vivid? It could not be better. Despite the dog's dark thoughts, the book is beautifully written in rhyming poetry that draws the reader in and evokes the most powerful of images instantly supported by the deliciously gruesome illustrations.

The bottom line: If we want students to talk about and respond to read-alouds, then we must give them something to talk about and respond to. They don't all have to love the selection, but they do have to consider it.

Today, many years, many read-alouds, and many responses later, I have not only considered *The Waiting Dog*, but I have come to love it. It is one of my must-have touchstone texts — I even have an autographed copy! *Lesson plan 2 in this chapter is based on this book.*

Modelling How to Explore Text Characters

Preparing an engaging read-aloud

Read-Aloud Plan 1
Selected Text: *Chester* by Mélanie Watt

Chester, a persistent, competitive cat, wants a story of his own so desperately that he takes over the author's story about a mouse. Entertaining and humorous, *Chester* can be used to support explorations of character, point of view, and use of visual and textual elements to make meaning. Told in two voices, it is a natural fit for readers theatre.

Select a "just right" text — our notes are based on *Chester* — and rehearse out loud. Practise how to differentiate the voices of the characters, in this case, author Mélanie Watt and Chester. If you think you need more than your voice, consider use of a mask, a puppet, or even cat ears to show when you are reading Chester's parts. Alternatively, invite a volunteer, educational assistant, or even the principal to read parts with you.

Prompting wonder, enjoyment, and thought about the text

Encourage students to look carefully at the front, back, and inner flaps of the book jacket. Use questions such as the following to engage students in discussion about the book. Draw their attention to Chester the cat. Ask: "What is he holding in his hand? What do you think he is going to do with that bright red marker?" If students don't notice on their own, show them that the author's name has been crossed off in bright red ink, with Chester's name written underneath. Ask: "When you look at the faces of Chester and the mouse, what do you wonder about or think?"

Read relevant parts to get students thinking about what the story might really be about. For example:

> *Front flap:* Hi I'm Mélanie Watt, and I'm trying to write and illustrate a story about a mouse. But Chester just won't stop interfering.
> *Back flap:* Forget what's-her-name . . . CHESTER is the real author and illustrator of *Chester*. Critically acclaimed by Chester himself . . ."

A Good Precedent: Talk About Text
"Much of the benefit — as well as of the child's enjoyment — comes from the talk that accompanies the sharing of the book. Discussing the characters and their actions, predicting what is likely to happen next, clarifying the meaning of particular words and phrases — all these kinds of talk help the child to make connections between the meanings and language forms of the text and his or her actual experiences, including the use of language in other familiar contexts." — Gordon Wells (2003, p. 3)

Focus attention on the back cover and ask students whether it gives any clue about the story ending. "Look at the mouse here. Is he feeling differently than he was at the beginning? What do you think might happen between the front cover and the back cover to make this change?" Record students' predictions and wonder statements on a chart to revisit later.

Read the story aloud to students.

At the end, ask questions such as these: "What do we know about Mélanie Watt/Chester? What is Mélanie Watt/Chester really thinking and feeling? What could Mélanie have done to make Chester behave? What story was the author really trying to share? Why did she choose to make Chester a cat?" Revisit the predictions and wonder statements. Invite students to say which statements they would change now that they know more. Ask students how they would feel if someone kept interrupting them or taking over their writing or conversation.

Capturing character perspectives through design

Revisit portions of the book and brainstorm with students the visual and textual elements the author used to communicate feeling, perspective, point of view, and meaning. For example, explore how design features (e.g., font, changes in font size, font color, and upper casing of words) affect story meaning. Ask: "Who writes in black? Who writes in red? Why?" Have students look at the detail within the pictures and comment on what the author is trying to say about the mouse's life and what Chester is trying to say about his life and those of Mélanie Watt and the mouse. How does the way the story is presented visually communicate meaning? Ask students whether they feel that the pictures and use of red revision carry more story than the printed text.

Exploring points of view

Point out that the reader never learns the mouse's point of view. Using shared writing (see Chapter 7), add in the mouse's point of view with sticky notes on the text. Negotiate with students an appropriate font, size, and color for the mouse's mood, feelings, thoughts, and words.

You can also use the sticky-noted book to create a readers theatre script that captures all three points of view. (As much as possible, use dialogue from the book.) Leave multiple copies of the script and a copy of the picture book at a readers theatre centre. Encourage students to explore the story in more depth.

Adopting the author's design tools in writing

Review the visual and textual design features that Mélanie Watt used in *Chester* to communicate meaning and portray character, point of view, and feeling. Encourage students grouped in partners or triads to write a collaborative story in the same style. For example, each student develops a character in words and pictures, and then uses font size, font style, color, and other design elements to portray the character's point of view. Remind groups that while Chester tried to hijack Watt's story, their task is to work together as a group to produce an entertaining story that can be shared with the rest of the class.

Provoking Student Reactions

We believe that simply reading aloud is not enough; we must also give students something worth considering and talking about. The books on our shelves satisfy the criteria for an effective read-aloud, but they also help our students make sense of their worlds, understand others, build character, and step outside their own realities into other times and places. We balance our literature selection to include texts that are real and imaginative; delight filled and wonderful; and as we must, tinged with tragedy and fear. In this way, we can share with students a little about how the world works.

A cautionary note about the value of such texts: Know your students well. You will know what they can handle and what they cannot. Assess them and ensure that the issues presented in texts are within their comfort and cognitive zones. Should the need arise, allow them to opt out during a read-aloud!

Setting up the experience

Select a "just right" text. In this instance, our model is *The Waiting Dog* and one week in advance, you can tell students that you will be reading a book that has a warning on the front cover: *Do you have the guts to read this book?* Build suspense each day, asking students to record questions, wonder statements, and predictions on a class chart. Whatever the title, set a purpose for listening.

Rehearse out loud on your own. Explore and practise appropriate volume, pitch, timing, and inflection. As always, the way you read the book will determine how students will react and respond to it.

"You don't have to like it,
But you have to consider it."
— *Mona Lisa Smile* (2003 movie)

Read-Aloud Plan 2
Selected Text: *The Waiting Dog* by Carolyn and Andrea Beck

As he waits, the dog imagines what he might do when the letter carrier arrives. Beautifully written in poetic style, this text is perfect to begin or end a unit on the human body.

Spell Weaving

Some books weave such a strong spell from front to back that it is not beneficial to interrupt during the first reading. *Owl Moon* by Jane Yolen is one. This enchanting book should be experienced purely for pleasure on the first read.

Decide how to handle the first reading, which is predominantly for pleasure. In *The Waiting Dog* a couple of stops are perfect for predicting (e.g., *Where do you think I would start?*). Do not plan too much; too many stops or questions will pull students away from the text. We recommend three stops as a general guideline.

Select an appropriate content text to read aloud just in advance of *The Waiting Dog* (e.g., *National Geographic*'s webpage about the digestive system). Doing this makes *The Waiting Dog* less jarring.

Just before reading, show and discuss the front cover. Encourage students to pay close attention to the warning, the illustrations, and the information. Are there any questions or predictions to add? Once the class has thoroughly discussed the front cover, show the back cover and read, "I sit and wait and salivate." Ask: "Does this change or alter your wonder statements and predictions?"

Sharing the text, garnering reactions

Read aloud with expression, enthusiasm, and appropriate intonation and pace, paying attention to phrases such as "I so love that little squirt, don't you?" Here are a few student reactions.

> As the read-aloud progressed, Mitchell gradually slid off his chair, paling as he went, holding on for dear life. When reminded that he could opt out of the read-aloud, he responded with mock indignation, "Nope, I have the guts to read this book."

> And another student, as the book came to a close, raised her hand and innocently asked, "Is this really appropriate for use in school?"

If the text is read without pictures, encourage students to visualize the words and sketch what they see in their mind's eye (often referred to as *sketch-to-stretch*). On the first stop, read the words, and then model how you would sketch your understanding or reaction to the text. Demonstrate that you do not have to be an artist to sketch what the mind's eye sees; instead, you can use symbols, conceptual words, color, texture, and intensity to convey how and what you are feeling. Stop one more time throughout the reading so that students can sketch their reaction.

Responding in a range of ways

Give students 5 to 10 minutes to think about and write their immediate reaction to the story. Remind them that they don't have to like it, but they have to consider it.

Divide students into groups of 3 or 4 to share immediate reactions, identify similarities and differences in their reactions, and explore the range of positive and negative reactions.

As a large group, discuss the text with an eye on content and information. Ask: "Is the story accurate? What is more fun to read — *The Waiting Dog* or a website?" Discuss story elements such as character, plot, and setting. Be sure to ask from whose perspective the story was told. (Surprisingly, according to Carolyn Beck, the story was told from the perspective of the letter carrier imagining what the dog might be thinking about.)

Reading as Risk Taking

When you debrief books such as *The Waiting Dog*, you will find that students are astute, honest, and eager to offer their views. Many will stand behind their view that few teachers would have the guts to read the book aloud — it is too risky! In their estimation, parents, other teachers, and principals would not approve of the dog's violent and aggressive thoughts, and that is reason enough to shelve the book.

Finally, choose from options such as these so that students can extend their comprehension, appreciation, and response to the read-aloud text.

- *Option 1:* Ask students to write 4 or 5 questions they would ask the authors to clarify their intent (see the More Ways section, page 60). Encourage them to follow up their question-asking by searching for responses on the Internet.
- *Option 2:* Direct the students to reread the text, experimenting with different rhythms, feelings, and expressions. Ask: "How does the way we read influence the way that we interpret and react to a story?"
- *Option 3:* Use *hot seating*, where a student plays a role, such as that of the letter carrier. The other students ask questions about the character's thoughts and feelings, and background; the student answers questions appropriately. Guide the students by asking good questions of your own. For example, if interviewing the letter carrier, you could ask, "What are the best and worst things about your job?"
- *Option 4:* Ask students to work in small groups to improvise a talk show that explores the perspective and point of view of the characters: the letter carrier, the dog, and the dog's owner.
- *Option 5:* In a large group, discuss questions, such as these: Why do we assume that the story is being told from the dog's point of view? Why do dogs have a bad reputation? Is it possible that dogs are more afraid of humans?
- *Option 6:* Encourage students to review the class's anchor chart for "just right" books, and write a letter to other teachers explaining why or why not the book just read is appropriate for a read-aloud.

Developing Effective Read-Aloud Experiences

"Reading aloud with children is known to be the single most important activity for building the knowledge and skills they will eventually require for learning to read."
— Marilyn Jager Adams

A Calming Experience
Reading aloud was always a life saver for us in the classroom, particularly for difficult-to-manage groups. Reading aloud always settled them and allowed us to find some common ground.

- Always read the book on your own before you read it aloud to your class to make sure that it meets your criteria for a "just right" book.
- Rehearse out loud: practise until you are comfortable with the words and can model appropriate phrasing, particularly with trickier texts. Experiment with how volume, pitch, timing, and inflection can alter meaning and the students' experience of the text.
- Be dramatic! Read with appropriate expression and intonation. Use different voices to mark the words of different characters. Remember: when reading aloud, you are modelling the behavior of a competent and confident reader.
- Establish routines for your read-alouds. If reading a picture book, you need to ensure that students are in a position to view the pictures — many teachers have a carpeted area in their classrooms where they can gather students or a document camera, where the picture can be projected for whole-class viewing.
- If reading a novel or a chapter book aloud, perhaps students can extend the act of listening and visualizing in their mind's eye to sketching to stretch their imaginations and comprehension. Not only does this provide a formal record of their visualizations, but these visualizations are immediate, do not interrupt story flow, and are not influenced by peer responses.
- Reserve time every day to read aloud to your students. Depending on book length, time could range from 10 to 20 minutes.
- Read books you love, sharing your enthusiasm and passion for reading with students. (Our list of favorite read-alouds appears at the end of the chapter.)
- Read aloud texts of many types — picture books, novels, news stories, poetry, website content. The possibilities are endless.

- After a read-aloud, make the text available to students at a literacy centre in print, audio, or computer-mediated forms. Many students will want to reread sections of the text, look at photos or illustrations, or maybe reread the entire text.
- Involve students in deciding what title to read aloud. (See "Making the Transition from Read-Aloud to Independent Text Choices.")

Making the Transition from Read-Aloud to Independent Text Choices

- Discuss with students why you choose specific texts to read aloud. Consider to what extent the following factors influence you: Does the text look entertaining? Have you read another book by this author? Does the text remind you of something or someone? Is there a lesson or content to be learned?
- Share with your students your strategies for choosing titles. Consider these questions: Do you look at the front cover? the number of chapters? the number of references? Do you read the first few pages to check on vocabulary or readability? Do you read reviews or do you read texts, website content, or articles recommended by peers? What do you do when you get into a text and don't care for it? Do you set it aside for another day or do you abandon it?
- Extend your selection of "just right" texts to student selection of texts to read independently; teach strategies such as the Goldilocks strategy or the Five Finger strategy detailed below.

Teaching Students How to Select "Just Right" Texts

One way to model literate behaviors is to extend consideration of text choice for read-alouds to the individual reading choices that students make. For both strategies outlined below, students choose a book they would like to read and begin to read it either aloud or in a whisper. Doing so will allow them to hear the places where they have trouble.

The Goldilocks approach

Selecting a book that is neither too hard nor too easy can be as difficult for your students as finding porridge, a chair, and a bed "just right" was to Goldilocks, that is, unless they have a strategy. Suggest that they use the following procedure and set of questions to help them find books that are "just right." This strategy works especially well with stories.

The student asks these questions while reading:

Too Easy
1. Have I read this book many times before?
2. Do I know and understand almost every word?
3. Can I read it smoothly and fluently without much practice or effort?

If "yes" is the response to most of these questions, the book is probably too easy. The student can still have fun reading the book, but next time, should choose one that is a little more challenging.

The student asks these questions while reading:

1. Are there more than a few words on a page that I don't recognize or know what they mean?
   (This strategy can be used in conjunction with the Five Finger strategy.)
2. Am I confused about what is happening in most of the book?
3. When I read aloud, am I struggling and does it sound choppy?
4. Is everyone busy and unable to help me if I hit a tough spot?

If "yes" is the response to most of these questions, then the book is probably too hard. The student can try it again later. By that time, the book may be "just right."

The student asks these questions while reading:

Just Right

1. Is this book new to me?
2. Do I understand most of the book?
3. Are there a few words per page that I don't recognize or know the meaning of instantly?
   (This strategy can be used in conjunction with the Five Finger strategy.)
4. When I read, are some places smooth and some places choppy?
5. Can someone help me with the book if I hit a tricky spot?

For more information, see:
"Lessons from Goldilocks: 'Somebody's been choosing my books but I can make my own choices now!'" by Marilyn Ohlhausen and Mary Jepsen in *The New Advocate, 5* (31–46) and *50 Literacy Strategies*, second edition, by G. E. Tompkins.

If "yes" is the response to most of these questions, then the book is probably "just right." Reading it will help the student grow as a reader.

The Five Finger strategy

This quick strategy helps students decide whether a book is too hard, too easy, or "just right." It works especially well with content books. Beginning with a raised thumb, students keep track of every word they find a puzzle. No fingers up means the book is too easy. More than five fingers per page means the processing of words is likely to interfere with the comprehension of text.

Monitoring for Learning

In the context of a read-aloud experience, observe whether students can do the following:

- make predictions or wonder statements and revise when prompted
- apply criteria to judge the appropriateness of a read-aloud
- consider perspectives and points of view different than their own
- consciously activate and apply prior knowledge and explain how it had an impact on their learning
- actively respond through talk, drama, or visual arts
- apply strategies that you have modelled and demonstrated to their independent reading

---

More Ways to Model Literate Behaviors

Create a language- and print-rich environment. For younger children, you can post poems or rhymes to help them make the connection between oral language and spoken language. Organize and label classroom resources and shelves,

For more information, see: "Grappling with Text Ideas: Questioning the Author," a 1993 *Reading Teacher* article by Margaret G. McKeown, Isabel L. Beck, and M. Jo Worthy (*46*, 560–566).

A home–school connection

"Children are made readers on the laps of their parents."
— Emilie Buchwald

helping students to make sense of all this print. For older children, you can post models of effective writing, checklists, or co-constructed anchor charts that serve as guides for poetry, drama, and storytelling.

While reading aloud, question the author's intent. Model how to stop throughout the text to explore and discuss the author's intent through questions such as these: "What is the author trying to say? Why do you think the author used the following phrase? Why did the author use this particular example? Does this make sense to you?" This strategy requires students to think about what the author is saying in addition to what the text states. It helps students build deeper-level understandings of text as they consider ideas in depth from the perspective of a writer and a reviser. It can be used with both narrative and content-area texts.

Help families to understand their role in modelling literate behaviors. Although many parents read to their children daily, they often need support to extend the read-aloud beyond simply reading cover to cover. During parent–teacher conferences or curriculum nights, show parents how to use sticky notes to plan two or three questions that they can ask their children while reading. You could even send home a picture book on which you have put three prepared sticky notes, with a quick note explaining the purpose of these notes. Encourage them to look for areas where they can make connections and extend the read-aloud into their daily life. For example, can parent and child co-construct a daily schedule after reading *Scaredy Squirrel* by Mélanie Watt? Can they draw a picture of what they like about themselves after reading *What I Like About Me!* by Jamie Lee Curtis? See the Home–School Connection line master on page 63.

> **Literacy Essential 5:** Reading aloud every day to every child a "just right" text that you enjoy and use to prompt critical thinking provides an excellent way to model literate behaviors; students can then follow your modelling to further develop as literate beings.

Texts That Make Good Read-Alouds

Books that are worth reading aloud are those worth talking about or those worth reading for the pure fun of it. At times, these texts allow students to explore realities similar to their own and to make meaningful and relevant connections; at other times, texts read aloud may provoke student reaction and allow students to consider realities and worlds unlike their own. Here is a short list of favorites.

"It is not enough to simply teach children to read; we have to give them something worth reading. Something that will stretch their imaginations — something that will help them make sense of their own lives and encourage them to reach out toward people whose lives are quite different from their own."
— Katherine Paterson

Picture books pertaining to change, gender, and diversity

Am I a Color Too? by Heidi Cole and Nancy Vogl (diversity)
Jenny Angel by Eve Bunting (death, courage)
Horace and Morris But Mostly Dolores by James Howe (gender)
Amazing Peace by Maya Angelou (conflict and peace)
Voices in the Park by Anthony Browne (socio-economic diversity)
Monster Mama by Liz Rosenberg (fear, courage)
Woolvs in the Sitee by Margaret Wild (fear, courage, change)
The Composition by Antonio Skarmeta (courage, politics, decision making)
Don't Laugh at Me by Steve Seskin and Allen Shamblin (teasing, empathy)
Skin Again by bell hooks (race)

The Boy Who Loved Bananas won the Blue Spruce Award offered by the Ontario Library Association for best Canadian children's picture book in 2006, as chosen by students from Kindergarten to Grade 3. In general, one good way of identifying "just right" books is by checking to see which titles have earned awards or popular appeal.

Why War Is Never a Good Idea by Alice Walker (conflict)
Caramba by Marie-Louse Gay (fear of being different)
Nokum Is My Teacher by David Bouchard
The Boy Who Loved Bananas by George Elliott

Picture books on multicultural themes

Very Last First Time by Jan Andrews (about an Inuit girl)
Orphans in the Sky by Jeanne Bushey (Aboriginal; set in the Arctic)
Red Parka Mary by Peter Eyvindson (contemporary Aboriginal)
Roses for Gita and *A Gift for Gita* by Rachna Gilmore (South Asia)
The Nutmeg Princess by Richardo Keens-Douglas (Caribbean tale)
The Orphan Boy by Tololwa Mollel (African Maasai legend)
The Always Prayer Shawl by Sheldon Oberman (Jewish traditions)
A Salmon for Simon by Betty Waterton (Aboriginal Canadian)
A Place Not Home by Eva Wiseman (refugee child from Hungary)
Mala: A Woman's Folktale by Gita Wolf (Indian folk tale)
Ghost Train by Paul Yee (Chinese Canadian)

Picture books for the pure pleasure of reading

No, David! by David Shannon
Monkeys in My Kitchen by Sheree Fitch
Olivia by Ian Falconer
Alexander and the Terrible, Horrible, No Good, Very Bad Day by Judith Viorst
Adventures of Cow by Lori Korchek
Click, Clack, Moo: Cows That Type by Doreen Cronin
The Stinky Cheese Man and Other Fairly Stupid Tales by Jon Scieszka
Goldilocks Returns by Lisa Campbell
Detective LaRue: Letters from the Investigation by Mark Teague

Novels

The Hundred Dresses by Eleanor Estes (socio-economic diversity)
Sadako and the Thousand Paper Cranes by Eleanor Coerr (war, loss, courage)
Underground to Canada by Barbara Smucker (slavery)
Naomi's Road by Joy Kogawa (Japanese Canadian internment in the Second World War)
A Very Small Rebellion by Jan Truss (Riel Rebellion)

Read-Aloud Tips and Strategies

Sharing books and reading aloud to your child is one of the best things you can do. Be sure to establish a read-aloud routine and to sit in a way that your child can see the pictures, turn the pages, and help you with the reading. Read and reread your child's favorites. Sooner than later, your child will join in on familiar parts or turn the pages at the correct time. You can even drop words and let your child fill in the gaps. But beware of trying to shorten up a lengthy tale — you'll get caught for sure! Don't be afraid to share your childhood favorites, offering memories as you read. Children need to hear that you have been a reader for a long time.

Before Reading Aloud

- **Read the story on your own.** Plan a few questions and record them on sticky notes; place one note per question on the relevant page (to a maximum of three).
- **Introduce the book to your child.** Read the title, look at the cover together, and ask: "What do you think the book will be about?" Make connections to the story by saying, "I remember reading this when . . ." "This reminds me of . . ."

While Reading Aloud

- **Encourage your child to chime in or take turns reading with you.** You can both use different voices for different characters. Put expression into your reading — your child will do the same.
- **Ask and discuss the questions you have prepared.** Here are some typical ones: "What do you think will happen next? What is happening in this picture? How is the character feeling?" If your child doesn't offer a response, say what you're thinking.

After Reading Aloud

- **Listen to your child's comments and notice reactions.** Say: "This is what you thought would happen . . . Were you right? Have you ever felt like . . .?"
- **Do something fun with your child to extend the story.** Draw a picture, make a model, act it out . . . have fun with the story in a way that helps your child to remember it.

Pembroke Publishers © 2012 *Balanced Literacy Essentials* by Michelann Parr, Terry Campbell. ISBN 978-1-55138-275-3

CHAPTER 6

A World of Texts for the Reading

Reading instruction . . .
More than a list of activities or description of strategies,
It's about how all the parts of our teaching can work together.
It's about helping children see connections and make new ones.
— Sharon Taberski, *On Solid Ground*

Reading is far more than decoding written symbols on a printed page — it is about the way we experience, interpret, and navigate our environment, the people we encounter, and texts of many types. In essence, our lives are laden with reading. Teaching students how to navigate a world of text requires a range of instructional strategies in addition to a solid understanding of students. We must shape our reading programs by addressing questions such as these:

- What do, and will, our students read? What purposes does text serve in their lives?
- What strategies and skills do readers require to succeed with texts of all types?
- How can we effectively guide and support our students as they make connections between how they read day-to-day situations and the strategies and skills they require to read texts of all types?
- What conditions support and foster purposeful and pleasurable reading of texts of all types?
- How can we promote a full command of reading comprehension, navigation, and critical thinking skills?
- What are the concrete conditions and practical strategies that make this learning possible?

What We Want for Our Students as Readers

"The ultimate end of instruction in reading is to enable the reader to participate intelligently in the thought of the life of the world and appreciatively in its recreational activities."
— William S. Gray

When we teach reading, we are aiming to provide students with strategies and skills that will enable them to navigate the world — not just the world of text — efficiently and effectively. Here, we are reminded of Frederick in Leo Lionni's tale of the same name. While the rest of the field mice gathered food and straw for the winter, Frederick appeared to be dreaming. Although he did not work in the conventional way, he was able to *read* the environment, the colors, and the needs of his friends and create a poem that transformed not only his existence but that of his comrades. This must be our goal for readers: for them to struggle and succeed with text in a way that allows them to navigate — and transform — their worlds.

In order to navigate a world of text, readers need to take on a number of roles — map reader, purposeful traveller, captain, and chartmaker — in order to crack the code of any particular text. In all roles, the reader needs to demonstrate continual awareness of personal reading strategies and processes.

Four Roles of the Reader

The Map Reader	The Purposeful Traveller
• Recognizes and uses a variety of word-solving strategies (including awareness of letter–sound relationships or decoding, word analysis, syntax clues, and context clues). • Draws on a repertoire of known words and symbols and continually develops a reading vocabulary that allows navigation of a variety of texts. • Recognizes and navigates language conventions (e.g., sentence structure, punctuation). • Recognizes and uses visual information as a guide to comprehension.	• Selects texts and reads in a way that permits travel to different times and different places for different purposes. • Is anchored in comprehension by knowledge of a variety of text features (e.g., story, poem, information). • Adjusts sails (reading strategies and reading rate) to match the text form and the purpose of travelling through the text. • Recognizes the author's voice in a text. • Travels successfully through a text by thinking metacognitively, connecting to previous voyages, and making meaning.
The Captain	The Chartmaker
• Establishes a purpose for navigating a text. • Recognizes that the journey — the purpose of reading — is the destination. • Recognizes that reading always involves travelling through a text in search for meaning. • Knows and sails through a variety of comprehension strategies. • Checks in and self-monitors while reading, recognizing when the route to comprehension breaks down and adjusts sails to restore it. • Sustains travel through text and comprehension, and maintains interest over an extended time. • Responds to texts in a variety of ways, adjusting sails when necessary.	• Recognizes reading as a transaction among reader, author, and reading community. • Explores, extends, and revises ideas, information, and perspectives in texts in order to help others travel to different times and different places for different purposes. • Engages in critical thinking, critical consciousness, critical literacy/inquiry in order to facilitate future voyages. • Recognizes points of view, omissions, and multiple perspectives of travellers and texts they encounter along the way. • Responds to texts in a variety of ways, discovering new worlds and charting new courses.

The plans that follow represent a range along the developmental continuum, from emergent readers, to early and developing readers, to fluent readers. While all include teaching through modelling, shared and interactive reading, and independent reading, in plan 1, the focus is on modelled reading; in plan 2, shared reading; in plan 3, guided instruction; and in plan 4, independent reading. Responsibility for reading and navigating text is released gradually as students become more skilled at charting their own courses through a world of text.

Exploring Text Depths Through Modelling

Reading Plan 1
Selected Text: *Stella, Queen of the Snow* by Marie-Louise Gay

Two children, Stella and Sam, engage in a question-and-answer dialogue about winter and snow. Sam's questions indicate his curiosity, but the pictures suggest he might be feeling apprehension. Students can explore Sam's inner thoughts and dialogue, and compare them to his visible dialogue, questions, behavior, and body language.

The subtext strategy (Clyde, 2003) provides students with the opportunity to "walk around inside a story — supplying characters' thoughts that are normally only implied by characters and their situations" (p. 150). This strategy allows students to make personal connections, relate to characters, and offer alternative perspectives based on their own experiences. It is important to choose a text that lends itself to exploring characters' thoughts, feelings, emotions, personalities, intentions, and motives.

Anticipating the destination

Read aloud the selected text once primarily for pleasure and to familiarize students with the characters and storyline. Before the second reading, mark spots to engage students in character think-alouds, and prepare a sticky note think-aloud for the first stop to model the strategy.

Modelling and testing the waters

Tell students that you will be modelling a strategy that will help them to better understand and empathize with characters; explain to students that sometimes what characters are thinking and saying are different. Begin reading the story a second time until you reach your first stop. Model how to stop reading, look at the pictures, make connections, and then write down what you think the character is really thinking. For example, at the beginning, when Sam is looking out the window, you might say: "Here, I'm thinking like Sam: 'Stella says it's snow. I've never seen snow before. I wonder how it feels.'"

Stop while reading, asking students to think like either Sam or Stella. Ask them to contribute further examples of what the character might really be thinking and to record their inner thoughts on small sticky notes. For example, a student thinking like Stella might say: "Wow! He sure does have a lot of questions! Why can't he just play in the snow!"

Exploring perspectives

Demonstrate to students how to organize their think-alouds into open-mind portraits (example for Sam is provided). Using a previous student's example, if available, demonstrate how these inner thoughts might be written into a script of what Sam is thinking.

Stella says when I look out the window I see snow. It looks cold. She says it's fun to play in, but I'm not sure. I have lots of questions. I wonder if she will be able to answer them all. I asked about a snowman. I'm a little nervous. She told me that they only eat pink snowsuits. I'm not sure I believe her. How can a man made of snow really eat a snowsuit and what would it taste like? I think of lots of other things that would taste better. We spent a lot of time outside in the snow today. I think I'm starting to feel better. I'm glad I made a snowman and listened for frogs. What I liked most of all was making snow angels and listening to them sing. I think I'm going to like winter a lot!

Make students' sticky note think-alouds for Stella available at the writing centre. Over the course of the week, encourage students to create a script that captures Stella's inner thoughts.

Relating to fellow travellers

Encourage students to think about what is going on in characters' heads when engaged in silent and independent reading. Support students as they make connections to their own lives, and discuss why what we think and say might differ. Brainstorm examples of when this might be a good thing or when it might be a bad thing. By contrast, you may want to engage students in shared reading with another text where a character effectively makes his or her inner thoughts visible — the poem "Today" by Jean Little is a good example.

The subtext strategy encourages students to empathize with characters and identify their thoughts, feelings, emotions, personalities, intentions, and motives. It may also help them relate to classmates with feelings different than their own, or children in other countries with different wants and needs.

Travelling Safely Through a Text with Shared Reading

Reading Plan 2
Selected Text: "Today" by Jean Little (from *Hey World, Here I Am!*)

The poem recounts a day where nothing goes right for a student. It allows students to make personal connections to it and provides a model for poetry creation.
The plan can be handled in four sessions.

Shared reading allows students to gradually wade into a text in a way that builds confidence and fosters joyful reading and student success. Teachers begin with a read-aloud of an enlarged text in small groups or with the whole class; the text is then extended into multiple readings, each one serving a different purpose. Successful travel through the text is charted by alerting students to key text features or tricky or unusual features. Students are encouraged to join in on the reading when they feel comfortable, thus apprenticing them into the reading community. As shared reading unfolds, you will gradually release responsibility for reading to your students. Your initial role is that of captain, but with each encounter with the text, students will become more comfortable, eventually assuming the roles of purposeful travellers and chartmakers.

Reading together for pleasure and prediction

You can enlarge your chosen text in one of a variety of ways, including big book format, overhead, SMART Board, and data projector. Identify the text's theme. Read the title and encourage students to make predictions about what they would expect to hear. Write predictions on a chart.

Read the enlarged poem aloud for enjoyment and the pleasure of being read to, pointing to each word as it is read (depending on grade level).

Check earlier predictions. Which were correct? Which were incorrect? Listen to student responses.

Prompt students to make connections between the poem and their own experiences. Ask: "Which of these statements would apply to you? What might your bad day sound or look like?"

> I remember the day I didn't want to go to school. I made a real fuss at home and then my dad was not happy about dropping me off at school. He got a speeding ticket on the way. Now that was a really bad day.

Addressing the tricky and unfamiliar

Invite students to look at the poem. Ask them which words are new and which they need to discuss and explore. Highlight words (e.g., *potential*, *enriched*, *contribute*), and have students predict what they might mean.

Read the poem aloud once, modelling that sometimes the strategy of reading on allows the reader to figure out what unfamiliar words mean.

Assign tricky words to groups of 4 or 5 students, and encourage them to consult various sources to define their word.

Gather students into the large group to share their definitions, and read the poem aloud once again; encourage students to join in when they feel comfortable.

Exploring ways to interpret the text

Discuss students' interpretations of the poem. What might have happened before and after the poem was written? What is the author really saying?

Distribute individual copies of the poem, and divide students into groups of 4 or 5, where they will experiment with how changes in tone, voice, expression, and volume affect the meaning of the poem (e.g., reading loudly might indicate anger, whereas reading with a slow teary voice might suggest sadness and frustration). Remind them that it is not always what they say, but how they say it that expresses meaning.

Allow small groups to present their interpretations of the poem, and ask other groups to identify the emotions in each reading. Discuss that no one interpretation is more correct than another and that, depending on experiences, all people will relate to the character in a different way.

Charting new texts

Ensure that all students have a copy of the poem, and explain that they will be using the poem as a model to write their own version using the structure "Today, I will not." Alternatively, they could write using the structure "Today, I can't."

Guiding Students in Reading

In guided reading, you work with small groups of students. Often, the students will have similar reading levels or require support with similar reading strategies. You can provide scaffolding and support them strategically in a way that fosters independent travel through increasingly challenging texts. Groupings for guided reading are flexible and purposeful, and always keep the student at the centre of instruction. Because students are grouped by both reading level and strategy use, students are able to read independently with a minimum of support and frustration.

When selecting texts for guided reading, consider the following criteria:
- The text is excellent children's literature with appeal, integrity, a good story, and vivid language. It is rich, true to life, not too moralistic.
- Everyone in the group can read it with the required rate of accuracy (between 90 and 95 percent).

Reading Plan 3

Selected Text: *The Snowy Day* by Ezra Jack Keats

This Caldecott Award–winning book, published in 1962, was instrumental in transforming children's literature. It recounts one African-American boy's absolute joy in the first snowfall of the season.

- The text supports demonstration of the strategy you want your students to acquire.

In the sample lesson plan, word endings are explored.

Introducing the book

Draw students' attention to the title of the book and the author's name. Students may give names of other texts they have read by the author. Ask students to predict what the story might be about by observing the cover illustrations. Say: "Let's look at the cover. What season is it? How do we know? . . . What is the little boy doing? What sounds might he be making?" Elicit sounds that snow might make as he is walking in it. Students may suggest words such as *crunch*, *crackle*, or *squeak* and find these words in the text; they can show their awareness of words by putting a finger in front and behind individual words as directed by you — "hugging" the word. Point at the footprints and ask: "What are these called? What do you think this story might be about?"

Highlighting tricky words

Go on a picture walk through the book, talking about the story found in the pictures and looking for ways to connect students' prior knowledge with the story. Scaffold important or new words, language, or structures found in the story by drawing students' attention to clues. Here is an example of what a teacher might say (italicized parts from the original text):

> (pp. 1–2) This little boy's name is Peter. One snowy day, he looked out the window. What did he see? He saw snow that had fallen during the night and covered everything. Let's find Peter's name . . .

Students should always be provided with character names during a guided reading session.

> (pp. 7–8) *Then he dragged his feet s-l-o-w-l-y to make tracks.* Let's look at this word carefully. What clue does the author give to tell us how Peter dragged his feet? That's right — he separates the letters in the word with hyphens. How do you think he wants us to read the word? That's right. He is suggesting that we read the word very s-l-o-w-l-y.

Here, we are alerting students to clues that authors use to direct the way we read.

Teaching to the almost known: Strategy work

The Snowy Day tells a story that has already happened — maybe yesterday. Explain to students that when someone is telling about something that has happened before, they often use *ed* at the ends of action words or verbs. Sometimes, they will also hear *ing* at the ends of words, represented by the letters *i n g*.

Guide and observe the students as each of them reads a copy of the book, keeping track of (and at times discussing) strategy use. Evaluate their use of strategies and their ability to read *ed* and *ing* appropriately.

Checking comprehension

Check earlier predictions, asking: "Were we right? What was in the story that we hadn't thought of?" Listen to student responses. Ask key questions to check comprehension too, for example:

> Retell: *What did Peter see when he looked out his window? What were some of the things Peter did outside in the snow? What sounds did the snow make?*
>
> Relate: *Tell about a time when you walked in the snow like Peter.*
>
> Reflect: *How do you think Peter would have felt if the snow had really melted away?*

Students will say things like: "Peter saw snow everywhere," "The snow made a crunching sound," and "I remember when I walked in the snow — it was fluffy and didn't make a sound."

Promoting Independent Navigation of Texts Through Response Tasks

Independent reading builds on the knowledge, skills, and strategies introduced during modelled, shared, and guided reading. This is your students' opportunity to demonstrate independent engagement with text and strategies on a variety of levels and to explore fully and navigate the four roles of the reader that you have been building through explicit instruction during modelled reading (read-alouds), shared reading, and guided reading. When teachers plan for independent reading, they acknowledge that people learn to be literate in collaboration with others; as they talk, explore multiple responses, and consider alternative interpretations, they grow in ability to navigate and chart new worlds and increasingly complex texts. Accordingly, teachers plan opportunities for students to engage in a combination of literature circles, grand conversations, reader response journals, readers theatre, and independent response activities.

Literature circles

For more information on literature circles, be sure to read *Literature Circles: Voice and Choice in Book Clubs and Reading Groups* by Harvey Daniels.

Literature circles are an effective way for students to read self-selected literature and talk about what they are learning about reading and writing. Literature circles are small groups where students accept responsibility for book selection, independent reading, meaning making, and group discussion of books. Small temporary groups are formed, based on book choice, with each group reading a different book. Groups meet on a regular schedule to discuss their reading, using written or drawn notes to guide reading and discussion. The goal is for students to engage in open, natural conversations about books that include personal connections, digressions, and open-ended questions. Initial experiences with literature circles often involve role sheets that focus students' attention on specific roles of the reader (e.g., map reader, purposeful traveller, captain, and chartmaker). As students gain confidence with literature circles, they will rely less on role sheets and more on their literacy notebooks or reader response journals.

Grand conversations

Grand conversations are discussions held by the entire class, informed by information gathered in literacy notebooks or reader response journals. They are similar to literature circles because both are student directed; what makes them different from literature circles is their focus. Grand conversations that focus on reading may address one specific piece of literature, specific story elements, or particular themes or genres. When you use grand conversations in the classroom, you allow for dialogue among students that is student directed; your students will have the opportunity to critique, debate, and extend one another's ideas. These conversations can be used to develop a reciprocal and recursive relationship between community building, talk, and understanding of literature.

Reader response journals

Sample Notebook Responses
"I guess the ant must not be too bright." (Luke's response to *The Midnight Fox* by Betsy Byars)
"I like that it gives voice. I like that it is intense. It is suspenseful. I think that everyone is going to get mad at him because he lied." (Michel's response to *The Lion, the Witch, and the Wardrobe* by C. S. Lewis)

Reader response journals are written records of student responses to readings, including immediate feelings and reactions, connections to one's life, other texts, and media, and reflections expressing opinions and critical analysis. The focus is on the development of the reader's interpretation and personal meaning-making, not on a single correct interpretation as dictated by a teacher or critic. Students may also comment on the author's process as well as their own process as a reader, essentially emphasizing the connections between reading and writing. In their notebooks, students keep track of interesting words, phrases, and ways of doing things that they might like to try as writers — encourage students to write about the things they like and dislike, as well as the things they find confusing, unusual, or funny. Students can use literacy notebooks, which cover reading and writing, for response too.

Here are two variations on open-ended journals:

- In *double entry* journals, readers choose quotations they find important and meaningful, record each quotation and page number in one column, and then record their thoughts and feelings in the right-hand column.
- In *dialogue* journals, two people reading the same book interact by means of the journal, responding first to the text, and then to their correspondent. Readers can converse with a peer, a teacher, or a family or community member. For example, when a student objected to vulgar talk that Tinker Bell used in *Peter Pan*, Michelann and she went on to discuss "thimble kisses."

Powerful Pauses for Response: Janet McIntosh

Writing responses during reading provides ideal opportunities for students to deepen and expand their understanding of literature. I've had junior-level students write journal entries as they read novels for literature groups, and I've observed that engagement in reading is the result. One classroom approach is to have students read an assigned portion of the text, and then pause, reflect, and write half-page responses at regular intervals.

Writing responses while reading is a key component of response journals. Initially, this practice can cause students some difficulty as they may feel that they are interrupting their reading to write. With time and practice, however, many realize that it's easier to record their ideas when the ideas are fresh in their minds. I've observed that pausing in the act of reading seems to spur them on to want to read more — as they move away from the text to write, they seem to be drawn back to it and want to return to their reading so they can gather more information.

Janet is an associate professor in the Schulich School of Education at Nipissing University in North Bay, Ontario.

Readers theatre

Readers theatre is highly motivating, especially for reluctant readers; it is a simple, effective, and low-risk way to foster enjoyment in reading. As drama through oral expression, it involves small groups of readers reading aloud prepared scripts and performing with purpose, using only their voices to convey the meaning of text. Eventually, students or small groups of students can be engaged in creating their own scripts. Readers theatre is not characterized by props, costumes, stages, or memorization of parts or lines. Its many benefits include collaborative group work, literary appreciation, greater confidence in oral language ability, increased vocabulary through repetition, and especially, reading fluency. Rasinski observes:

> What would really inspire me to engage in repeated reading or rehearsal is performance. If I were to give an oral reading performance of a passage, I would most certainly have an incentive to practice, rehearse, or engage in repeated readings. All of us, at one time or another, have read orally for an audience. It is likely that we practiced in advance of that reading, and if we didn't it is likely that we wish we had. To continue with this line of reasoning, if performance is the incentive to practice, then we need to ask what kinds of texts lend themselves to expressive oral performance . . . (2006, p. 305)

The kinds of texts used in readers theatre, as well as interactive poetry, chants, dialogues, and rhymes, can be easily read aloud with expression and understanding. Rasinski concludes, "To me these texts are the perfect fit for fluency instruction and repeated readings" (2006, p. 305).

Self-directed response activities

Response-based approaches move beyond literal examination of the text to focus on student engagement and construction of meaning through interaction with texts, other readers, and classroom contexts, facilitated by use of literature circles, grand conversations, literacy notebooks, reader response journals, drama, and storytelling. Students respond to texts by reflecting on their own emotions, attitudes, beliefs, interests, strengths, and personal experience, and then relating these to the text. For example, response activities can be planned around the multiple intelligences in order to facilitate student response and engagement.

Selected Text: *Lesia's Dream* by Laura Langston

This historical novel recounts the story of a young Ukrainian woman as she immigrates to and settles in Canada with her family. It talks of the struggles and hardships of working the land, dealing with death and imprisonment of family, as well as learning to read and write a foreign language. Students are eager to discuss Lesia's experiences and can relate to a character who works hard to belong in both her family and her new country.

Intelligence	Story Element	Response Activity
Linguistic	Character Plot	Write a series of letters that might have been sent back and forth between Lesia, her mother, and her father while they were imprisoned.
Logical-Mathematical	Plot	Keep track of the sequence of events from the beginning of the book until the end (for example, before they left the Ukraine until Lesia's marriage in Canada).
Musical	Setting	Research the traditional music of the Ukraine and its transfer to Canada. Choose a passage of text and create a musical score or soundscape to accompany its reading.
Bodily-Kinesthetic	Character	Create a series of tableaux, or frozen pictures, that represent Lesia's working of the land. What kinds of strengths and skills would she have needed?
Spatial	Character	What are the relationships between Lesia and other characters? Create a *character sociogram* (a graphic representation of relationships using pictures, symbols, shapes, colors, words, and even line to show the nature and direction of her relationships).
Interpersonal	Character, Plot, Setting	Engage students in literature circles or grand conversations about the story.
Intrapersonal	Character, Plot, Setting	Become Lesia and write a journal from Lesia's perspective as she settles in Canada. How does her life differ from yours? How does hearing about her life help you to understand yourself?
Naturalist	Setting	Use RAFT writing (based on Role, Audience, Format, and Topic) to write a set of directions from the land to Lesia, telling her how to clear and maintain it. (See Chapter 7 for more.)

Guidelines for Successful Instruction in Reading

1. Recognize that student independence as "real readers" is the ultimate goal.
   - Guide students to choose their own texts (see Chapter 5).
   - Emphasize reading as a process that emerges and grows the more we read.
   - Balance direct instruction, guided instruction, and independent learning with a focus on what happens before, during, and after reading.
   - Provide strategic and just-in-time support as students are engaged in guided or independent reading.
   - Use frequent student conferences to give feedback, guidance, and encouragement.
   - Show students how to monitor their own processes and progress.
2. Emphasize reading and writing connections all the time. Critically examine literature to learn about how authors write, and how they influence the reader.
3. Provide multiple purposes for reading — for example, to find pleasure, to be informed, and to perform a task with opportunities to apply comprehension and meaning-making strategies.
4. Use high-quality literature and texts of many types in multiple contexts: reading and thinking aloud, independent reading, shared reading, literature circles.
5. Emphasize the collaborative nature of reading by including many opportunities for discussion and interaction (e.g., grand conversations, literature circles, small-group response).
6. Give students plenty of time to read at their instructional level and within their interests; build uninterrupted, sustained, silent reading (USSR) and opportunities for oral reading into every day.
7. Provide explicit instruction in word solving that builds word knowledge (e.g., awareness and analysis) and teaches skills and strategies for word solving (e.g., structural analysis, context clues).
8. Use a variety of assessment techniques to inform instruction (e.g., reading journals, conferences, reader response tasks) and relate reading instruction to children's previous experiences.

Reading Assessment Across the Learning Continuum

Assessment in reading is largely dependent on the context within which you choose to assess. Regardless of the context (e.g., read-aloud, shared reading, guided reading, independent reading), the purpose of reading assessment is to observe students as they develop their sense of selves as readers and apply increasingly complex strategies to navigate texts of many types.

Read-Aloud: As students read aloud, encourage them to think aloud so that you can assess their in-the-head thinking and share the strategies that they use. This will enable you to discuss and reflect on effective strategies, often teaching to the "almost known" as you help them to solve a particular problem or give them something new to try.

Shared Reading: You can evaluate and assess students engaged in shared reading as you conference with them one-on-one or in small groups, listen to them read a portion of the text, or listen to them retell the story. You can also evaluate students' awareness of sight words, letter–sound relationships, and sentence structure. When they make errors, the students have opportunities to correct and apply fix-up strategies to their reading. You can use a variety of recording

If you seek training in conducting and scoring running records, check out eWorkshop, which is Ontario's Education Foundations program sponsored by TVOntario: www. eworkshop.on.ca. There is an excellent training program and e-learning module. Marie Clay's *Running Records for Classroom Teachers* is an excellent desktop reference.

and assessment plans (e.g., journals, anecdotal notes, checklists) for activities and strategies that were used by students.

Guided Reading: Assessment of guided reading provides significant information for subsequent planning and instruction; it concentrates mainly on the readers' acquisition and application of problem solving, using meaning and grammatical cues, as well as letter, sound, and word knowledge. You will know that you are using guided reading successfully when you see your students develop self-extending reading systems that allow them to become flexible and proficient problem solvers and readers. The level of student learning in guided reading is assessed through observation before, during, and after reading, predominantly through running records. Running records enable teachers to assess each student individually, paying close attention to their use of strategies and comprehension of the text.

Independent Reading: Assessment takes place predominantly through conferences, review of reader response journals/notebooks, observation of students engaged in dramatic reader responses, storytelling, and literacy centre work in response to texts they are reading independently, sitting in on literature circles, and listening in on grand conversations. Text below provides tips applicable to a few key assessment forums.

Assessment tips pertaining to conferences

When you conference with students about reading, be sure to do the following:

1. Listen to familiar reading that they have selected first, prompting appropriately and judiciously.
2. Talk about the story idea or topic; have a real conversation (try not to interrogate the reader). Think about whether your questioning style is interview, comprehension check, or dialogue. Plan questions that assess different types of thinking.
3. In some cases, you will also use a reading conference to formally assess students with running records. When this happens, begin with a familiar text and then introduce a new text. The student then reads aloud as you listen, observe, and record, taking a running record with notes on "how it sounded."
4. At the end of the conference, (1) give specific praise at the cutting edge of the reader's learning (e.g., a strategy tried for the first time, a noticeable improvement in fluency, a skill recently mastered), (2) teach the almost known (choose one teaching point, based on an observation of the reader trying something, but not quite "getting it"), and (3) assign further reading that is at the student's instructional level and of interest to the reader, trying to make the decision collaboratively.

Question Prompts for Different Kinds of Thinking

The following sample prompts are based on Bloom's well-known taxonomy: knowledge, comprehension, analysis, application, synthesis, and evaluation.

Knowledge	Application
Who, what, when, where, how . . . ?	How is ____ related to . . . ?
List three . . .	What inference can you make?
Do you recall . . . ?	What is the function of . . . ?

Comprehension	Synthesis
What facts or ideas show . . .? What is the main idea of . . .? Can you explain what is happening . . .?	Can you propose an alternative . . .? Suppose you could ____, what would you do . . .? Can you think of an original way for the . . .?
Analysis	**Evaluation**
What other way would you plan to . . .? Can you make use of the facts to . . .? What questions would you ask in an interview with . . .?	Do you agree with the actions . . .? How would you prove/disprove . . .? What choice would you have made . . .?

Assessment tips pertaining to literature circles and grand conversations

As you assess the effectiveness of literature circles and grand conversations with your students, consider the following factors: the level of discussion that occurs, students' growth as readers and writers, and how well your students follow the established rules for participants' social behavior.

1. Either sit in on the discussion or videotape/audiotape individual literature circles over the course of a book or grand conversations with multiple texts. Use these tapes with groups to talk about the type of discussion, the overriding themes, the ability of the group to remain on task, the positive and negative elements of the discussion, and individual student contributions.

2. Individual students and groups can self-assess using checklists or rubrics you have negotiated with students. Criteria may include establishing a schedule for reading, completing reading on time, fulfilling reader responsibilities, bringing book to literature circle, and participating productively and respectfully in discussions.

3. Look for a wide range of reader behavior, including understanding of literature, student interaction, critical thinking, and understanding of literary content. For detailed assessment strategies and examples for literature circles or grand conversations, consult *Moving Forward with Literature Circles* by Jeni Pollack Day, Dixie Lee Spiegel, Janet McLellan, and Valerie B. Brown.

Reflecting on practice

Finally, but no less critically, reading assessment involves reflecting on who we are as teachers of reading. Considering the following questions will help to inform our practice:

- What skills and strategies did the students learn and apply? What opportunities for additional practice do they need?
- Was the text selection appropriate for the purpose of the lesson?
- Does text selection and response to students demonstrate respect for students as individuals with unique cultural backgrounds, families, and life experiences?
- How did the instructional strategies support student acquisition of selected skills and strategies?

Instructional Strategies for Readers Who Struggle

While the continuum of support that we have described works for all students and accommodates most students, there is no one-size-fits-all solution for readers, particularly for those who struggle to read, for whatever reason. This underscores the need to be close observers and assessors when adapting or readjusting instruction to meet the diverse needs of learners with exceptionalities, English Language Learners, or students with cultural differences. Before offering specific instructional strategies, though, let's consider the general needs of readers who struggle:

- They need to read a lot in order to build stronger vocabulary and use of strategies.
- They need books that they can read: readers must be matched with texts at appropriate reading levels.
- They need to be internally motivated to read: voluntary engaged reading is linked to greater skill as a reader.
- They need to read fluently, which, in turn, leads to automatic information processing and higher-level thinking.
- They need to become thoughtful and critical readers who can navigate texts of many types.

For more information on the use of text-to-speech technology in the regular classroom, see "The Voice of Text-to-Speech Technology: One Possible Solution for Struggling Readers?" by Michelann Parr. It appeared in *What Works? Research into Practice* in June 2011.

Specific strategies that have proven to be effective with students who struggle with reading include these:

- repeated readings, assisted by teacher read-alouds, shared reading, paired reading, audio-books, and text-to-speech technology
- modelling and demonstrating how to handle reading a tricky text through think-alouds
- a combination of read-alouds, shared reading, and guided reading
- readers theatre (especially for development of fluency; see Chapter 9)
- use of cooperative groupings, including small-group, large-group, and partner activities, so that all feel a need to participate
- introduction of graphic and advance organizers for reading (e.g., graphs, webs, timelines, Venn diagrams, story maps)
- picture walks before reading to activate prior knowledge
- predictable, readable texts with supportive illustrations, at the readers' level
- sensitivity to idioms, multi-meaning words, homophones, and other language peculiarities
- return to books to discuss difficult or tricky language structures
- adoption of the whole-part-whole method (reading the whole book, returning for individual parts, and then rereading the whole book)
- self-selected reading on areas of personal interest
- choice of books at students' reading level
- pre-reading scaffolding to make text more accessible; willingness to provide texts in multiple languages, if needed
- individual conferences to work on specific areas of need
- use of sticky notes to mark confusing/unfamiliar words and structures
- encouragement for students to build their own word dictionaries (adding illustrations when appropriate)
- "Every student" response activities, for example, holding up YES/NO cards or making finger symbols
- open-ended activities with multiple response formats

- use of the concepts of multiple intelligences and learning styles to plan for students
- creation of a print-rich classroom, with clear and useful postings (e.g., lots of labels, text, environmental print, sentences, questions, word walls, in multiple languages if needed)
- use of pictures, illustrations, real objects, and other visuals
- bringing in of objects your students will encounter during lessons and guided reading
- use of manipulatives, such as magnetic letters, word cards, and pocket charts
- establishment of positive home–school relations

More Strategies for Exploring Text and Promoting Reading

Because different texts require different navigational practices, teachers must have a large bank of strategies at their fingertips; having this will thereby allow them to support students individually and in small groups as they discover, explore, and chart new texts. The following strategies are those we have found most useful.

Hold book talks. Book talks are intended to entice students to read books recommended by teachers, parents, librarians, and peers. They can be teacher developed or student generated. They are like quick advertisements or brief commercials for a book; they talk about the book without giving away the ending. Presenters tell why they chose it and what they liked about it. Book talks should take only one to two minutes.

Explore Question–Answer Relationships (QAR). QAR is a strategy that helps students to realize that there is a relationship between the question asked and the answer found. QAR (Raphael, 1984; 1986) teaches students that answering different kinds of questions requires different reading behaviors, different sense-making strategies, and different thought processes. Some questions require students to find an answer in the text, explain something they have read in their own words, elaborate and make connections, or evaluate their own thinking and sense-making about a given topic. Confronted with questions, students must be able to read a question and determine where they are likely to find the answer, whether they are using books, videos, media presentations, or websites. There are four categories of questions that students must become aware of during strategy use and practice.

For more information, see these articles by Taffy Raphael:
"Teaching Learners About Sources of Information for Answering Comprehension Questions," in *Journal of Reading* (*27*, 303–311).
"Teaching Question–Answer Relationships," in *The Reading Teacher* (*39*, 516–520).

QAR: Applied to *Hero Cat* (Eileen Spinelli)

Right There	Think and Search
The answer is in the text, so you could point at it and say, "It's right there!" *Signal words:* who is, where is, list, when is, how many, when did, name, what kind of	The answer is in the text, but you might have to look in several different sentences or places to find it. *Signal words:* summarize, what caused, contrast, retell, how did, explain, find two examples, for what reason, or compare
For example: *When did Hero cat realize the kittens were in danger?*	For example: *What caused the fire in the abandoned building?*

Author and You	On My Own
The answer is not in the text, but you still need information that the author has given you, combined with what you already know, in order to respond to the question. Inferences fall into this category.	The answer is not in the text, and you don't even have to have read the text to be able to answer it.
For example: *How do you think the mother cat feels when she realizes that the building is on fire?*	For example: *What are possible reasons for Hero cat being a stray cat?*

For further information, see *Content Area Reading: Literacy and Learning Across the Curriculum* by Richard T. Vacca, Jo Anne L. Vacca, and Deborah L. Begoray.

Implement anticipation guides to help students to explore what they already know and understand about given concepts. Particularly effective in content-area reading, they help students build a framework for new learning and connect new knowledge to existing knowledge. Their use allows the teacher to engage students in active and critical thought before, during, and after reading.

Before: Identify the major concepts or topics in the reading that you would like students to consider. Create 5 to 10 statements that will require students to challenge, investigate, and discuss what they already know or understand about the concept. Anticipation guides can use a true/false, before/after, agree/disagree, or open-ended response format (see "Fact or Fib" in Chapter 9 for an example). As each statement is read, they must justify their thoughts, opinions, and responses, drawing on previous knowledge and experience. Statements are revisited once research and/or reading is complete.

During: Engage students in reading. As they read, prompt them to focus on collecting new information that either supports or refutes the statements introduced.

After: Return to the original anticipation guide and read it through statement by statement, engaging students in discussion. If students have changed their mind, they must provide new information from the text that justifies their new thoughts, opinions, and responses. Encourage students to compare their initial responses to their understanding after reading.

Home–school connections

Promote reading by sending "I Can Read" books home. Since these texts have been used for shared reading in the classroom, students can read them independently and with confidence. The more they practise, the better they get and the more fluent their reading becomes. The books can be sent home weekly with a list of activities that parents can do with their children (e.g., ask your child to "hug" specific words, play I Spy giving hints of the words to find). The key is that students have already mastered the texts in the collection. All they have to do is focus on fluency and celebrate what can be read independently with their families.

Provide book bags to help parents support their children. Book bags each contain a book and any items that might be useful in retelling or talking about the story or text. These bags may also contain activities or games that can be completed at home with parents. Book bags can be designed to focus on specific concepts (e.g., about print). All materials necessary should be included in the bag. Teachers often have one per student to rotate each week throughout the year. The idea is to enhance parent–child interaction.

Favorite Texts That Support Students in Reading

Texts such as these can be used to help children understand the roles of the reader and what reading is all about:

- *The Pagemaster* (adventure fantasy film available on DVD; the ultimate reader response)
- *The Neverending Story* by Michael Ende (available as print text and on DVD; connection making)
- *Jeremiah Learns to Read* by Jo Ellen Bogart (never too late to learn to read)
- *I Hate to Read!* and *I Still Hate to Read!* by Rita Marshall (persuading and engaging reluctant readers)
- *Reading with Dad* by Richard Jorgensen (the importance of talk and encouragement in reading)
- *Thank You, Mr. Falker* by Patricia Polacco (determination of one teacher to help one student read)
- *Junkyard Wonders* by Patricia Polacco (about struggling readers and writers)
- *The Wednesday Surprise* by Eve Bunting (never too late to learn to read)
- *Wolf!* by Becky Bloom (motivation to read)
- *Leo the Late Bloomer* by Robert Kraus (reminder that some take longer to get there)
- *It's a Book* by Lane Smith (reading in today's world of technology)
- *Charlie Cook's Favourite Book* by Julia Donaldson (making connections between familiar texts)
- *The Three Pigs* by David Wiesner (making connections between familiar texts)

Here is a list of our favorite books to use along the continuum of support; unless noted, these books can be enjoyed by students of any grade.

Reading aloud for pleasure

Picture books

The True Story of the Three Little Pigs by Jon Scieszka
My Lucky Day by Keiko Kasza
The Jolly Postman by Janet and Allen Ahlberg
The Kissing Hand by Audrey Penn (primarily primary)
Miss Rumphius by Barbara Cooney
Frog and Toad Together by Arnold Lobel
Officer Buckle and Gloria by Peggy Rathmann
Fly Away Home by Eve Bunting
Diary of a Worm by Doreen Cronin
Imagine a Day, Imagine a Night, and *Imagine a Place* by Sarah L. Thomson

There by Marie-Louise Fitzpatrick

Novels

Mr. Popper's Penguins by Richard and Florence Atwater (available on DVD)
Abel's Island by William Steig (available on DVD)
Charlotte's Web by E. B. White (available on DVD)

Shared/Interactive reading

Any text from a poetry anthology or written by the class will do because you can reproduce it without breaking copyright. For example:
- *So Cool* by Dennis Lee
- *Hey World, Here I Am!* by Jean Little
- *Science Verse* by Jon Scieszka

Chapter 8 features a detailed list of our favorite poetry anthologies. Alternatively, choose a text available in big book format with a repetitive pattern or structure. For example:
- *Red Is Best* by Kathy Stinson
- *The Very Hungry Caterpillar* by Eric Carle
- *The Doorbell Rang* by Pat Hutchins

Independent reading and literature circles

Most of these titles would be read by junior students.
Lesia's Dream by Laura Langston
Ticket to Curlew by Celia Barker Lottridge
Shadow in Hawthorn Bay by Janet Lunn
Owls in the Family by Farley Mowat
Shiloh by Phyllis Reynolds Naylor
Tales of a Fourth Grade Nothing by Judy Blume
Ramona Quimby, Age 8 by Beverly Cleary
Tuck Everlasting by Natalie Babbitt
The Tale of Despereaux by Kate DiCamillo
Because of Winn-Dixie by Kate DiCamillo
Bridge to Terabithia by Katherine Paterson
Family Under the Bridge by Natalie Savage Carlson
The Great Gilly Hopkins by Katherine Paterson
Maniac Magee by Jerry Spinelli
Sarah, Plain and Tall by Patricia MacLachlan

CHAPTER 7

Writing to Be Read

Children want to write. They want to write the first day they attend school. This is no accident. Before they went to school they marked up walls, pavements, newspapers with crayons, chalk, pens, or pencils, anything that makes a mark. The child's marks say, "I am."

— Donald Graves

The realities of everyday life see our students experiencing, creating, and engaging in a wide range of imaginative and informational texts for multiple purposes. As teachers, we are constantly seeking ways to guide our students through oceans of texts in ways that will encourage them to accept literacy challenges from very young ages throughout their lives. We want them to experience the joys of simple handwritten notes and the exhilaration of exciting multimedia presentations. Most important, we want them to be able to confidently and successfully put their mark on the world.

The processes involved in creating original texts seem sometimes hidden and mysterious. Think of the Leo Lionni character Frederick, who has apparently just been dreaming for days on end. Once he triumphantly presents his dramatic poem about the seasons, he entertains and *impresses* his comrades ("Why Frederick," they said, "you are a poet!"). This experience is ultimately what we want for our students: the joy of creation, of proudly sharing it with their community, and receiving recognition and applause for their efforts and accomplishments.

Yet when young Daniel was involved in an early literacy intervention program for Grade 1/2 students, he had this to say:

> Mrs. Campbell, writing is *so much harder* than reading. When you read, it's all there for you already — you just have to figure it out. But when you have to write, you have to start from nothing!

So, how do we teach, guide, and support young writers as they chart their journeys into the unknown, progressing from "nothing" to something? This chapter provides key teaching strategies designed for learners all along the developmental continuum, from emergent to fluent writers, and includes how to provide a continuum of support, from teacher modelling to interactive and shared writing, to productive independent writing activities in the context of a literacy workshop. It also includes a plan for integrating phonics and word solving (sound, letter, and word knowledge) for emergent learners into the workshop setting.

The Writing Challenge

Just as reading is more than decoding, writing is more than encoding. As noted in Chapter 6, when readers learn how to make sense of text, they can be viewed as orchestrating four interconnected, complex roles: map reader, purposeful traveller, captain, and chartmaker. The same roles can apply to writing, with those of captain and chartmaker taking on greater prominence. Young writers coordinate the roles as they compose their own texts.

1. As map readers, writers "solve" words using a variety of strategies, from the letter–sound analysis required for encoding to the drawing on of automatically known vocabulary ("instant words," learned through repeated writing and reading in various contexts).

2. As purposeful travellers, writers navigate a variety of forms to express ideas, thoughts, and feelings; to convey information; and to record imaginative creations. They use appropriate language conventions and syntax learned through oral language and reading texts. They develop a metacognitive awareness of author's voice and how to write with a specific audience in mind.

3. As captains, writers establish purposes for writing — self-monitoring and checking that they are staying the course, and correcting their writing with readers in mind.

4. As chartmakers, writers engage in the ultimate role, as they embark on self-directed transactions between themselves and their readers, other authors and other texts, and the reading–writing community. They understand writing as a process that involves charting journeys through rehearsing, drafting, revising, editing, and sometimes publishing. Taking on multiple perspectives of the travellers and texts they encounter along the way, they recognize their use of point of view and its effect on the reader. They write to inform and entertain, inviting readers to discover new worlds and plot new courses.

The ultimate orchestration of these four roles occurs when one writes like a reader and reads like a writer. For the author, this entails writing with the reader in mind as one reads and rereads one's writing.

The potential of writers' workshops

Good Sources on Writers' Workshops
Check out *The Writing Workshop: A World of Difference* by Shelley Harwayne and Lucy Calkins and *Writing Workshop: The Essential Guide* by Ralph Fletcher and JoAnn Portalupi.

As with reading instruction, a continuum of support, from explicit teaching through modelling to shared and interactive writing to independent practice, applies to writing. We should also consider how the writing process has been adapted in response to the use of newer technologies for writing, from using spelling and grammar checks for editing to using software to create media works. A literacy workshop with a focus on writing is a good context for showing how writing instruction has evolved.

The order behind apparent chaos

Writing Program Features
1. *Writing for:* showing students how it's done using modelling and demonstrating
2. *Writing with:* doing shared and interactive writing
3. *Writing by:* providing "places to go and things to do," as Lucy Calkins puts it, for independent writing

When we think about literacy workshops that focus on writing, we recall the essential elements that must be in place in order to foster engagement and success for all. We pay particular attention to what these elements would look like and sound like in writing:

Walk into Liz McArton's Grade 5–6 classroom during her writing workshop, and you will see students all over the room, in the hallway, and on a nice day, just outside the classroom door. Some of them are writing scripts using a word-processing program, some are rehearsing the narration of their stories in small groups, some are taking digital photographs to include in their media presentation, some are creating costumes and props with construction paper, scissors, and glue. One student has completed a media work using iMovie and is showing another how to use the editing features to create special effects. "It may look like chaos," says Liz, "but they all know what they are doing!"

The following represents the order behind apparent chaos.

- *Mini-lesson:* The first part is a literary warm-up, where the teacher may tell or read a story to stimulate ideas or provide a model text, engage students in choral reading of a poem to inspire poetry writing, or work with students on a short piece of writing interactively. The second part is explicit instruction (modelling) based on student need. Topics could include conventions, such as punctuating dialogue or paragraphing; writer's craft, such as sentence combining, writing good beginnings and endings, and using "juicy words"; and revising and editing skills (by hand or word processing). Ten to 15 minutes is enough.
- *Status of the class:* The teacher circulates with class list, recording who is at rehearsal, drafting, revising, editing, and publishing stages. Two or three minutes are enough.
- *Writing time* (with time for talk): In phase 1, students orally rehearse with a partner for 5 to 10 minutes — in other words, they write aloud. In phase 2, they engage in sustained independent writing for 25 to 30 minutes. The teacher circulates or conducts conferences while they do this.
- *Authors' sharing time:* Students present works in progress for audience feedback and group problem-solving. Work can be at any stage of the writing process, including oral rehearsal. Ten to 15 minutes is recommended.

Word Soundings

This plan offers a whole-class approach for reinforcing letter, sound, and word knowledge, using explicit instruction as well as shared and independent practice. The generic approach can be used in the classroom in the context of the literacy workshop with learning centres incorporated. The same routine, flexible activities, and sequence can be employed cyclically. Altogether, students do about 30 minutes of sound, letter, and word work a day. The plan takes a multiple intelligences, multi-level, multiple learning style approach.

Establishing starting points for word solving

Observe and keep anecdotal records to track student growth in word solving: read their daily writing, listen to their oral language, read with them, and listen to them reading aloud.

Write-Aloud
An oral rehearsal gives children the chance to put what they want to say into words before they write it. They later read their writing aloud after writing to help them "hear" what their writing sounds like.

A Way to Impress Their Friends
Grade 3 teacher Michelle Hlusek reports that ever since she began to routinely include what she and her students call "Authors Share," she has observed a marked improvement in motivation to write interesting pieces.

Writing for, with, and by

Writing Plan 1
Focus: Exploring phonics and word solving, especially for emergent learners
Suggested time frame is five days.

This plan can be adapted for older students to establish, review, and reinforce key spelling patterns (e.g., *tion* in *nation*, *ight* in *light*). By adapting the sequence, you can create spelling charts or word wall lists interactively with your students and post them for their reference when writing.

Introducing, studying, and reinforcing individual sounds

Isolate the sound. Brainstorm with students as many words as possible that have a particular letter, sound, or spelling pattern. Listen to the sound, decide as a group whether it fits the pattern, and then look at the way it is written. Sometimes, as with *f* and *ph*, we enter into a group discussion that the /f/ sound can be made by *ph* and then we look at words such as *telephone* and *elephant*, substituting *f* for *ph* to which they all respond, "That doesn't look right!" As each word is written, individual students can add a picture cue to the chart. These charts can be posted around the room as guides for writing.

Choose a key word to anchor the sound. As a group, choose the word you like best or use most often. That word becomes your key word for the sound (e.g., *elephant* for *ph*). Ask the students (each taking a turn) to come up and underline the targeted sound in one word on the chart, reinforcing the sound with the visual representation. Take all the words they have and make a class visual dictionary page with the key word much larger than the others. In the next session, they can illustrate and underline the targeted sound on their own page (a great transition activity).

Use the sound in a meaningful way. As a follow-up, encourage students to use as many of their brainstormed words as possible to create a humorous picture. Circulate as they are drawing and write their sentences interactively with them (e.g., *Philip and the elephant were talking on the telephone*). In preparation for the sentence centre, review the sentences and words they have used, and create sentence strips for each student that reinforce the sight words, the key word selected, and the words they can read independently.

Use the sound in shared reading and shared writing. Introduce a poem, short text, song, or joke, and engage the students in a shared reading experience. The text selected should contain the sound being studied. While studying the /ph/ sound for example, you could use the Raffi song "Willoughby Wallaby Woo" (an elephant sat on you!). Use the text during transitions and reading-the-room activities with the goal of reading it independently after multiple rereadings. Once the students can confidently negotiate the text, engage them in shared writing to create a new stanza or verse. Encourage small groups to rehearse the stanzas for presentation at week's end.

Use centres to reinforce sound work. Students can independently rotate through centres similar to the following for an hour (15 minutes per centre is more than enough in early primary). Small groups not requiring the same level of intervention could be engaged in guided reading or mini-lesson work with the teacher. Ideally, a volunteer can help supervise.

- Computer centre: Students use KidPix or another computer program to find and stamp words or pictures that have the targeted sound or letter.
- Word study centre: Students sort the word cards they find in the box by sounds they hear and say.
- Sentence centre: A volunteer works with students as they cut apart, scramble, and unscramble the sentences recorded on rectangular strips, glue them into their books, and illustrate them. The complexity of sentences is varied depending on the level of students.
- Magnetic letters centre: Students manipulate magnetic letters on cookie trays, matching upper and lower case letters, creating words with the targeted sound/ letter or spelling pattern. For stronger visual effect, they can use an overhead projector to see the letters and words, and practise writing them.

"... it is the ownership of words that gives one confidence."
— Courtney B. Cazden

When reading and writing are taught simultaneously, young children use "common sources of information since there are processing connections that must arise in the learner who is being taught to read texts of many kinds and to write texts of many kinds by the best instruction currently advocated."
— Marie Clay (1998, p. 137)

Writing for: Exploring modelled writing

"An artist paints with his class, a science teacher illustrates the art of investigation and documentation, and a coach shows how she spreads her fingers to control a basketball. Good teaching means demonstrating the decisions and skills required to participate in the field of study or endeavour being taught. This also applies to writing."
— Donald Graves (2005, p. 1)

Writing Plan 2
Focus: Using a mentor text to examine story structure

Selected Text: *Marianthe's Story: Painted Words/Spoken Memories*

Marianthe's Story, by Aliki, is based on the author's experiences of coming to America from Greece. It has a definite beginning, middle, and end.

Celebrate and consolidate the learning. Hang the brainstorming poster up with the others as a record of learning, creating a learning or audit trail. Students each choose their favorite piece of work and read a sentence from it; then, each small group presents its interpretation of the shared reading text.

Making the Thought Behind Writing Visible

When students observe teachers writing in front of them, talking about their writing as they go, they learn that even the writing of "experts" often begins tentatively, untidily, and undergoes a process of many decisions about word choice, punctuation, deletions, additions, mistakes, and corrections. Without active demonstration of how writing is accomplished, it remains invisible and mysterious. Effective teaching of writing means lots of modelling of the processes of writing, with special emphasis on showing the invisible processes that make communication through writing possible. By writing aloud, you can show what a writer does and articulate how a writer thinks.

In addition to demonstrating good writing through your own modelling, you can offer models of good writing by established authors, displaying and discussing examples of different kinds of texts, including a wide range of forms and genres. You can show students how to be constantly on the lookout for examples of how to express ideas, learning, and feelings through stories, poems, letters, and informational texts.

When using a text as a literary model or mentor, ensure that it is very familiar to the students. When *Marianthe's Story* was used in a Grade 3 class as a model for how to shape a personal story, it had been read aloud twice the previous week and read independently by most of the class. In this case, the students had got as far as listing possible writing topics, but had not yet begun drafting stories.

Warm-up — Talking about the theme

For the literary warm-up, ask the students to turn to a partner and talk about a time when they were the *new kid* (e.g., first practice with a new soccer team, first day in a new classroom). Use a prearranged signal for the changing from teller to listener at the midway point.

With a previously prepared BME (Beginning, Middle, and Ending) chart, engage in explicit teaching or modelling using "I" statements.

> Today you are going to learn more about how to shape your memories into a story. You know that a good story has a beginning, a middle, and an ending. I am going to show you how I use a good story as a model for my own story writing. I am thinking about Part 1 of *Marianthe's Story: Painted Words*. I notice that the author has the book organized into three parts, like this:

Show the three headings of the BME chart: Beginning, Middle, Ending.

> I am going to write one sentence that summarizes the beginning of the story, one for the middle, and one for the ending . . .

Beginning	Middle	Ending
Mari prepares for her first day in her new school, telling her mama that she is worried that she won't understand anyone, and they won't understand her.	Mari paints her story every day in her new classroom during "creating time," from her family in the old country, to her struggle with name-callers, and the teacher who helped her.	Mari shows all of her paintings during Sharing Time, and her classmates and teacher applaud her.

Once you have filled in the chart, say something like:

> I could use this as a plan to make sure my story has a strong beginning, middle and ending. I could then add details to each section. Then I will have a complete story plan, and I can begin to write a draft.

Provide paper or computer (word processing) template; guide the students to fold the paper or create the three-part chart, and tell them they will be writing one sentence under each heading, based on one of their topics.

Guided and independent practice

Write-Aloud: Ask students to turn to a partner to talk about which topic from their list they plan to write about; they then write one sentence under each of the three headings. Have them turn back to their partner to share BME charts and ask each other questions. Partners can discuss what details they will add to each part of the story.

Writing Time: Prompt students to add details: two to the Beginning, at least three to the Middle, and two or three to the Ending.

Sharing Time: Provide time for students to share how they are organizing their stories through the BME chart; let them ask for suggestions and feedback from their peers. Explicitly tell the students that in the next mini-lesson you will focus on drafting. They will learn how to draft a story based on the planner and have time for writing aloud, drafting, and sharing.

Extending the learning — mentor texts

During a read-aloud, pose any of the following questions to reinforce the use of mentor texts as literary models:

- What do you think about how this author tells a story?
- What does this author do that you would like to do as a writer?
- Which is a sentence in this book you wish you had written?
- Point out a sentence you would read aloud to your family or friends.

You can model the ideas in any of these questions by referring to texts you are reading for enjoyment.

> I [Terry] have been reading *Half-Blood Blues* by Esi Edugyan. Sometimes I read a sentence that just stops me in my tracks, like this one:
> *Anxiety hung over the streets like clothes on a line.* [page 220]

Checklist: Is This Mini-Lesson Effective?
- Is there one focal point?
- Is the lesson brief and direct?
- Do I explicitly tell students what they will be learning and why I am modelling it?
- Do I scaffold new learning by building on what they already know?
- Do I use ongoing assessment to guide lesson topics?

"A successful writing program requires a knowledgeable, organized teacher with excellent classroom management skills. Mostly, students need lots of time in which to write, a say in what they write about, strategies that allow them to problem solve independently (plan, revise, edit), and helpful response."
— Regie Routman (2005, p. 173)

Exploring Shared/Interactive Writing to Compose and Revise

Shared writing differs from modelled in that the students do the composing while the teacher does the recording on chart paper, overhead, or interactive whiteboard. In interactive writing, students share the pen, contributing familiar words, ideas, letters, and sounds; this works particularly well at the revision and editing stages. Please note, however, that lots of modelling happens in shared and interactive writing! Celebrate and revisit the texts created. Perhaps read them chorally, post them in the classroom or in the school, or send copies homes. Students are always interested in rereading their own creations on topics they have chosen.

> **Possible Forms Shared/Interactive Writing Can Take**
>
> | | |
> |---|---|
> | Lists, clusters, and concept webs | Persuasive pieces and advertisements |
> | Story maps or organizers for writing | Science experiments and diagrams |
> | Timelines | Scripts for plays or readers theatre |
> | Letters and personal narratives | Reports, recounts, and summaries |

Drafting guidelines through shared writing

Writing Plan 3

Writing with . . . : An anchor chart to guide writing time

Suggested time frame is two days.

Read or experience something together to warm up and become inspired (e.g., your text about how to solve problems at recess).

Brainstorm possible topics or introduce the topic you have selected for the day. Here, our focus is on creating an anchor chart to guide class time for writing so that it is quiet and productive. Discuss possible guidelines, starting the students off with a positively worded statement, such as *Use quiet voices.* Reach a consensus on each sentence, writing it on chart paper or other easily readable surface. In shared writing, the teacher records while students assist by telling or writing known words, letters, or sounds. Reread each sentence as you go. Continue drafting until the class has no more ideas to offer.

Reread the whole text together. Leave the text on the stand, and invite students to think about what to add. Explain that they will be revisiting the guidelines on another day.

Revising and editing interactively

This session builds on an earlier one where, with the teacher as scribe, the class composed an anchor chart listing guidelines for their independent "time for writing." It is presented as a re-creation.

The teacher says: "Yesterday we created a list of guidelines on the chart stand for making our time for writing quiet and productive. Let's read it aloud together." The class reads aloud the guidelines, and then the teacher notes that one student, Aisha, added a sentence: *Don't talk to me when I am writing!* The teacher invites the class to go through the text line by line "and see if we would like to fix or change anything."

Line 1: Diego notices the spelling error and goes up to the chart with a blue marker, stroking out *quite* and writing *quiet* above it.

Line 2: All agree it is okay.

Line 3: Trinity wants to add the word *quiet* between *own* and *writing*. She uses the inverted *V* symbol and writes in the word above the line.

Line 4: Tanya notices that the *n* in Writer's notebook should be capitalized.

Added line: Sam notices that the other guidelines say "you" but this one says "me." Aisha, who added the line, is given the chance to reword it. She offers:

Don't talk to anyone who is writing alone at the writing centre.

Added line: All agree it is okay.

The teacher invites the class to read the chart together and decide whether any more changes are needed. The class reads aloud the short text, with corrections.

Guidelines for Time for Writing

quiet
Use ~~quite~~ voices.

Sit side-by-side or in a small circle when talking about your writing.

quiet
Use one of the writing centres for your own∧writing.

N
Keep all your writing together in your Writer's ɴotebook.

Don't talk to anyone who is writing alone at the writing centre.

> "Our students need what readers and writers the world over need. They need places to go and things to do."
> — Lucy Calkins

The teacher then arranges to publish the new version (preferably with the class or a small group of students). The finished anchor chart is posted and referred to just before independent writing time.

Writing Assessment That Is Rooted in Connections

Writing assessment involves looking at the connections that students make between what they read and what they write. Questions such as the following can guide not only the assessment of students, but review of the writing program.

- Do students make connections by using relevant prior knowledge before, during, and after reading and writing?
- Do students identify main ideas or themes as they read and write, and distinguish between important and unimportant information?
- Do students use prior knowledge, reactions, and information to judge, evaluate, and compare texts that they have read and written?
- Do students read between the lines to seek answers to questions, draw conclusions, and create interpretations that deepen understanding of the text? Do they apply inferences from mentor texts to their own writing?
- Do students enjoy and play with the aesthetic features of language when reading and writing (e.g., rhymes, rhythms, metaphors)?
- Do students predict and generate questions, revisit questions, and clarify meaning before, during, and after reading and writing?

- Do students react to or become emotionally involved with what they read and write and describe what makes them love, hate, or can't stop reading or writing?
- Are students aware of when they understand and when they don't? Do they self-monitor and self-correct? If they have trouble writing specific words, phrases, or longer passages, do they use a wide range of problem-solving or fix-up strategies (e.g., referring to the word wall or personal dictionary, consulting with a peer editor, or reading their writing aloud)?
- Do students summarize by tracking main ideas as they read and write, retell details in their own words, focusing attention on what is important?
- Do students create a wide range of visual, auditory, and other sensory images as they read and use this information when writing?

Effective evaluation and assessment involves
- frequent oral feedback as the teacher circulates during writing time
- focus on one or two error-types at a time during student conferences, where teaching correct forms can occur on-the-run
- full evaluation of only a few polished pieces, chosen with the student as representative samples of "best work" kept in a cumulative folder or portfolio
- consideration of growth over time
- student self-evaluation and self-assessment

The Most Useful Assessment Tools
- Literacy notebooks or writing logs for keeping track of works-in-progress and finished pieces
- Checklists for the various writing process stages
- Rubrics for completed work
- Observational notes, made during large- and small-group instruction, and individual conferences

To encourage self-assessment, ask one or two questions during a conference, for example:
- Why did you choose this topic? What makes you care about it?
- When you read your writing out loud, does it flow?
- Is there a catchy introduction? Does the conclusion leave the reader thinking?
- Do the events follow in an order the reader can follow?
- Is your train of thought clear? Are there any parts that don't belong?
- Is a vivid picture created in the reader's mind?

Then send the student off with one useful suggestion for revising or editing. During an individual conference, be sure to praise something specific about the student's writing.

Finally, but no less critically, writing assessment involves reflection on who we are as teachers of writing. To inform our practice, we are wise to consider questions such as these:
- What skills and strategies did the students learn and apply? What opportunities for additional practice do they need?
- How did the instructional strategies support student acquisition of selected skills and strategies?
- Am I effectively modelling all phases of the writing process? (For ease of reference, see the chart.)

Supporting Students Who Struggle with Writing

In addition to technological programs, scribing, peer support, collaborative small-group work, and individual conferences, it may be necessary to provide small-group mini-lessons to some students. Through use of specific strategies,

"[R]emember that students need to spend most of their time writing independently. If they are to become excellent writers they have to spend most of a writing lesson composing continuous text, not participating in lessons and activities about writing."
— Regie Routman (2005, p. 75)

you can give support to those who may be reluctant writers or who have problems with writing:

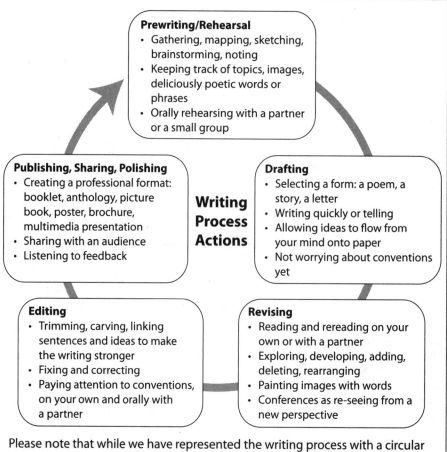

Prewriting/Rehearsal
- Gathering, mapping, sketching, brainstorming, noting
- Keeping track of topics, images, deliciously poetic words or phrases
- Orally rehearsing with a partner or a small group

Drafting
- Selecting a form: a poem, a story, a letter
- Writing quickly or telling
- Allowing ideas to flow from your mind onto paper
- Not worrying about conventions yet

Revising
- Reading and rereading on your own or with a partner
- Exploring, developing, adding, deleting, rearranging
- Painting images with words
- Conferences as re-seeing from a new perspective

Editing
- Trimming, carving, linking sentences and ideas to make the writing stronger
- Fixing and correcting
- Paying attention to conventions, on your own and orally with a partner

Publishing, Sharing, Polishing
- Creating a professional format: booklet, anthology, picture book, poster, brochure, multimedia presentation
- Sharing with an audience
- Listening to feedback

Writing Process Actions

Please note that while we have represented the writing process with a circular graphic, we recognize that writing is quite recursive. At any stage, students are free to go back and orally rehearse or draft again, revise, edit, or share. With the advent of computers, students often carry out these actions simultaneously on screen without great awareness of what they are doing or why they are doing it. It is up to us, as teacher, to support our students as they navigate this complex process and bring together all that they have learned in oral language, reading, drama, storytelling, and poetry.

- Provide more structure, guidance, and monitoring.
- Explain expectations for writing and feeling that they are a part of a community of writers.
- Arrange lots of modelling, demonstration, and levels of support.
- Set short-term, achievable goals during conferences. Use task analysis when necessary: help the students identify the specific bits that need attention, perhaps use of quotation marks in dialogue.
- Encourage students to select topics that interest them.
- Make sure that their audience extends beyond you as teacher.
- Provide multiple opportunities to work on the same piece of writing.
- Incorporate writing into larger culminating project posters, visual arts, and games.
- Select writing projects that have specific purposes and that capitalize on students' strengths.

- Make sure that resources are always in the same place.
- Encourage 10 minutes of free writing to loosen up and let ideas flow.
- Offer choices of where to write, how to write, what to write, and who to write for.
- Encourage students to read and enjoy texts in formats they want to write in, perhaps poems, letters, or comic strips.
- Brainstorm, rehearse, discuss in advance.
- Use concept webs, charts, story maps, and organizational frameworks.
- Have frequent, regular writing conferences and Sharing Time with open questions about the writing, not just feedback. For example:

    Why did you choose this topic? What makes you care about it?

    What do you like about what you have written?

    What will your next step be?

    Are there any other characters you could introduce?

    What kinds of things would they say to each other?

    Do you have a beginning, a middle, and an ending?
- Encourage student feedback and conferencing before, during, and after writing.

Guidelines for Peer Feedback: TAG

Tell what you like.

I like your description of . . .
I think the words . . . are interesting because . . .
I like the ending because . . .
I like it when the main character . . .
I think it is interesting when . . .
I like the part where . . .
I like it when you say . . .

Ask questions.

How did the . . .?
Who is the . . .?
Where will the . . .?
Why did . . .?
What happened to . . . ?
What made you decide to . . .?
Where did you get the idea for . . .?

Give suggestions.

I think it would be more exciting if . . .
You could add more information about . . .
I would like to know more about . . .
Your ending might be more interesting if . . .
Perhaps you could tell more about . . .

Zeroing in on individual needs

- Experiment with page positioning for students. (To reduce the movement of the page or book, for example, tape it to the desk.)
- Provide individualized word walls and alphabets.

- Provide a pencil grip for students with poor fine-motor coordination — elastics work well. Larger pencils, markers, and crayons also have a different feel.
- Provide cues of where to write, for example, happy face, arrow, highlighting (for those who have trouble with spatial orientation).

More Strategies for Writing Well

Depending on your circumstances and experience, you can either use the ideas below to extend your repertoire of strategies or to confirm strategies you already use.

Teach the concept of a sentence, and how to write one, using favorite sentences as models. To paraphrase Stanley Fish (2011):

> Alone, a word is just a word, a part of speech . . . it looks over at other words it would like to have a relationship with [like dating]. A verb shows up, providing a way of linking noun to adjective, and suddenly you have a sentence, a proposition, a little world.

Two favorite sentences:

> It was in the books before it was out of the park. — John Updike

> A blanket of snow was laying itself down, exhausted from the fall from the clouds. — Grade 5 student, 2010

John Updike's sentence (cited in Fish, 2011) is about a record-breaking home run in Fenway Park; it stops you while reading and makes you think: a model for writing.

Guide students on how to break text into paragraphs. Paragraph writing is a skill that junior-level students grow into as they gain experience with reading. Still, we can provide a guide, reinforced through mini-lessons, prompting students to create a new paragraph when there is a change in any of the following:
For non-fiction writing: a change in topic or subtopic
For fiction writing: changes in the five *P*s — Person speaking, Point in time, Place, Plot direction, Point of view

Introduce RAFT writing, whereby students adopt a certain point of view.
Role of the writer: Who are you as a writer?
Audience: For whom are you writing?
Format: What form will your writing take?
Topic: What are you writing about?
When engaged in RAFT writing, students adopt a specific role from a real life, literature, or content-oriented context and write from that perspective (for example, a fictional character, an animal, an expert in a content area). RAFT writing assumes a viewpoint or perspective different than the student's, an audience other than peers or teacher, and a form different than those typically used (reports, essays). A writer, for example, may take on the role or viewpoint of a plant, writing a letter to the sun to thank her (warmly) for her role in allowing her to flourish, grow, stay green, and bloom.
Role — plant; **Audience** — the sun; **Format** — letter; **Topic** — thank you

Helping Young Writers Find Their Voice in Writing: Jeff Scott

I have found that students are able to use their voice when researching something of interest to them. In the primary grades, animals are always a popular area of research. I introduced students to frameworks, a tool that is effective for gathering and organizing information effectively on a single page. The use of this tool combines the skills of deciding what information is necessary, how much information is needed and relevant, and point-form note taking, as well as the organization of the final paper, sentence construction, and the composition of each paragraph. The following is an example of a framework.

Heading 1: Penguins	
Criterion 1: Appearance Criterion 2: Flight Criterion 3: Classification Criterion 4: Interesting Facts	sharp beaks, smooth belly waddles, can't fly, have solid bones bird family spiky tongues, Emperor Penguin is the largest, Blue Penguin is the smallest

The piece of writing below is the third of three paragraphs on penguins produced by a Grade 2 student. It has been edited only by a peer! Notice the student's use of voice.

. . . Guess what animal category a penguin fits in? If you guessed birds your right. Lots of people think that penguins are in a different category because they can't fly. Just because they can't fly doesn't mean that they can't be in the bird category. My feelings got hurt when the penguin book that gave me the facts told me that almost every person in South America didn't think that penguins were in the bird category.

Jeff is an associate professor in the Schulich School of Education, Nipissing University, North Bay, Ontario. He was a Grade 2 teacher when the student wrote this.

Home–school connections

The Important Thing
The important thing about the family fork is that you eat with it. It might be silver or gold, maybe even wood. It might have your name written on it or it might not. It makes your food easier to eat and a whole lot less messy. It sometimes brings more colour to your food and usually makes it taste better. . . . But the important thing about a fork is that you eat with it.

Promote shared writing at home through travelling tales of journey animals. Send home a backpack that contains a stuffed animal, such as a blue monster; a book to share; a digital camera; a journal; crayons and pencils; and an explanatory note. Over a three-day period, families document their experiences with the journey animal and create a journal entry. Students then share their entries and answer questions during Sharing Time. Be sure to model a journal entry before sending home a backpack.

Send home travelling texts — books with a certain structure — to foster shared writing at home. Provide a copy of a model such as *The Important Book* by Margaret Wise Brown. Ask students and their families to respond with a related family story in a journal. Other travelling text activities might be to invite families to enter a new stanza to a poem, a new recipe to a book, or a favorite experience. Entries can be shared each day in the classroom. A sample entry by a junior teacher appears at left.

Literary Models That Demonstrate Aspects of Great Writing

"The point of surrounding students with wonderful literature and engaging them in conversations about what makes those pieces work, is for students to internalize the process and begin making connections on their own."
— Shelley Harwayne

The following titles are presented according to the aspects of writing they best exemplify. They can be used as mentor texts at various stages of the writing process.

- Choosing an engaging topic (*Puffins Climb, Penguins Rhyme* by Bruce McMillan)
- Creating stories with lively characters, well-sequenced plots, and believable settings (*17 Things I'm Not Allowed to Do Anymore* by Jenny Offill)
- Shaping personal narrative — oral to written, past to present (*Marianthe's Story: Painted Words, Spoken Memories* by Aliki)
- Creating mood (*Salt Hands* by Jane Chelsea Aragon; *Owl Moon* by Jane Yolen)
- Coming up with a good title (*What's a Penguin Doing in a Place Like This?* by Miriam Schlein)
- Composing (and punctuating) good dialogue (*Stella, Queen of the Snow* by Marie-Louise Gay).
- Creating a circular plot (*Where the Wild Things Are* by Maurice Sendak)
- Using repetition effectively (*Brown Bear, Brown Bear, What Do You See?* by Bill Martin, Jr.)
- Keeping it simple (*Grandfather Twilight* by Barbara Berger)
- Persuasive writing (*Don't Let the Pigeon Drive the Bus!* by mo willems)
- Writing with a love of words (*Max's Words* by Kate Banks)
- Creating a narrative from a newspaper account (*Hero Cat* by Eileen Spinelli)
- Choosing strong verbs, descriptive adjectives, and a variety of nouns (*Every Single Night* by Dominique Demers)
- Encouraging individual voice or "using a different kind of pencil" (*Omar on Ice* by Maryann Kovalski)
- Using visual images to stimulate descriptive writing (*The Mysteries of Harris Burdick* by Chris Van Allsburg)
- Gathering words and weaving them into stories (*Max's Words* by Kate Banks; in book and video format)
- Revising respectfully (*Chester* by Mélanie Watt)
- Writing graphic stories (*Diary of a Wimpy Kid* by Jeff Kinney)
- Carrying a story through images (*The Invention of Hugo Cabret* by Brian Selznick; in book and video format)
- Believing in ourselves as writers (*Library Mouse* by Daniel Kirk)
- Creating images with simple text (*Only Opal: The Diary of a Young Girl* by Barbara Cooney)

CHAPTER 8

Play with Language as Earprint: Poetry

In our fast-paced, "instant everything" world, we need poetry. It helps children and adults to ponder, to observe, to ask questions, to discover sights, sounds, and feelings that otherwise might remain untapped. It brings balance and beauty to our increasingly complex world. Poetry can awaken our senses or bring the element of surprise into our lives. It makes us laugh, teaches us powerful lessons, and renews our souls.

— David L. Harrison and Kathleen Holderith (2003, p. 6)

Poetry, often the first genre heard by children, is rooted in oral tradition. As children journey into literacy, they often encounter poems such as those by Mother Goose, Dr. Seuss, Jack Prelutsky, and Dennis Lee. Those repeated often enough become part of a child's repertoire — we can often hear a poem or song in the background as children play. If children can sing or recite a poem, chances are they will soon be able to read it, sooner or later writing poetry of their own — a natural response. Traditional nursery rhymes are a good place to begin.

Teaching Poetry

"When she reads some poems she slows down and kind of does actions and descriptions with them, so it's like . . . real. When the people turned into stone she kind of made it slow and we could see them turning into stone and it was brilliant — I love her reading poetry aloud."
— Toby, age 6 (quoted in Cremin, Mottram, Collins, & Powell, 2011)

Teaching poetry begins with reading and speaking poems aloud in a way that makes the words leap off the page straight into the hearts and minds of listeners. That can be easy to do because poetry is fun and rhythmic, well able to engage and captivate students' interest. To write a single poem, you have to have read and listened to many poems. In *Poems Please!* David Booth and Bill Moore recognize the oral nature of poetry:

> Poetry is earprint. It longs to be said aloud. It plays with language and with the sounds and rhythms of language. Very young children know about poetry. They clap along, sing along, and join in with rhymes that are hundreds of years old. We can bring poetry to the ears of our children in many ways. It is the constant ear training that will bring children to see the need for poetry. (1988, p. 72)

And yet, for many, teaching poetry can be intimidating, perhaps due to less than positive memories or experiences with poetry over the years, perhaps due to what many of us experienced as over-analysis and deconstruction of poems. We are not alone in this trepidation; even authors such as David Booth have had moments struggling through the how, why, when, and where to teach poetry:

The poem "What Will I Teach?" from *Poems Please! Sharing Poetry with Children* (Pembroke Publishers, 1988, page 136), is used with the express permission of the author, David Booth.

What Will I Teach?

I live in fear
    that I
    will teach the poem
    and they
    will lose the poet
    and the song
    and the self
    within the poem

I live in fear
    that I
    who love the poem
    and the children
    will lose the poem
    and the children
    when I teach the poem

But I will teach the poem
    Live with the fear
    Love the children
    Sing the song
    Find the self
    And know the poet
    is beside me
    Just as afraid
    But full of hope.

For us, poetry is so important that it forms the basis of one of our literacy essentials. Far beyond the aesthetic pleasure of experiencing a great poem or the joy of using language in playful ways, poetry has many benefits:

- It creates opportunities to play with language, one of the key principles of literacy learning.
- It fosters awareness of the sounds of language through rhyme, rhythm, and repetition, to enjoy those sounds, and to use this knowledge as a tool in becoming literate, and developing as literacy learners.
- It can build immediate success with students, allowing them to focus on the fun and joy of creative writing unencumbered by structure, grammar, and punctuation.
- Multiple readings of poetry (through modelling, shared reading, independent reading, and even reciting during transition times) develop fluency and expression, and support students as they develop awareness of letter–sound relationships and vocabulary. With each reading, students find increasing levels of comfort within familiar words.
- Poetry can be read in many different ways for many different purposes, thus making it a natural fit with differentiated instruction.
- Poetry allows teachers to connect reading, writing, and talk in meaningful ways with an eye on language and word play, word choice, and word order.
- Poetry can help students to both learn and demonstrate learning of content in fun, interesting, and non-traditional ways

The Waiting Dog by Carolyn Beck (illustrated by Andrea Beck) and *Science Verse* by Jon Scieszka (illustrated by Lane Smith) are examples of poetic texts through which students can learn content and demonstrate their learning.

Exploring All a Poem Has to Offer

To explore poems with your students, you will need poems and poetry anthologies of all types: nursery rhymes that are easily recognized by students, poems written by contemporary authors students can relate to, songs of today's generation (the poems most familiar to older students), poems that allow exploration of word choice, word order, rhyme, and rhythm, and poems that can be used as models for students' own thoughts, ideas, and voices. For specific suggestions, see "Poetry Texts for Children" at the end of this chapter.

Before engaging in poetry with your students, spend some time exploring your poetic self. Consider these questions:

• Do you like to write poetry? Why or why not?
• What poems do you remember from childhood?
• What do you remember about learning poetry?
• How comfortable are you with poetry?
• What do you think are the purposes of poetry?
• How might you work with students who haven't experienced nursery rhymes and finger plays at the preschool level?

Your responses and feelings to these questions will have a direct impact on what you do in the classroom.

What if . . .
we started each day with a poem
poems lasted all through the day
poems just were.

Poetry — Something We Did in the Classroom: Michelann Parr

One of my favorite anthologies is *The Random House Book of Poetry for Children* (compiled by Jack Prelutsky and illustrated by Arnold Lobel). It was one of the first books I bought for my own children, well loved and well read almost every day. When I began to teach, it always sat on the corner of my desk (much to my children's dismay). It never failed to provide me with a poem for my pocket or a poem to post for shared reading each day. My students would encounter poems every day as they "read the room," as well as hear the ones I used during transition times. We talked about the poems, we drew pictures about poems, we recited poems to music, and we experienced the magic of poetry. Poetry was something that we did in the classroom.

Push Push Push
Fasten Seatbelt When Seated
Use Seat Bottom Cushion for
Flotation
Push
Passenger Safety Information
Push
Airfone — Stay in touch with your
world when you fly in ours!
Exit Push
Exit Exit Exit

Familiarize yourself with children's poetry. Read it aloud often, seeking poems that offer beauty and simplicity in their use of words and that leave you with a sense of comfort. Explore the many poetry websites on the Internet. Write a poem — write, read aloud, revise, share! Students will want to know that you write poetry too! Pay attention to words and phrases in the environment. Found poems are a great place to begin. Non-threatening and fun, they often capture an experience. They are created by choosing direct quotations, random phrases, or words from a variety of genres, texts, and formats to create an original poem. Phrases and words are manipulated and pieced together in a way that creates a strong and powerful image. For example, the poem at left was "found" on a flight to San Antonio.

Poetry Lesson Plan 1
Selected Text: "Alligator Pie" by Dennis Lee

This poem satisfies all the criteria related to exploration: it has clear structures and repetitive patterns that we can discuss with students; it is entertaining and engaging, it lends itself well to drama, and it is easily used as a mentor text to create new stanzas and poems.

Preparing for poetry

Select a poem that offers many opportunities for exploration — rhyme, rhythm, drama, rewriting, dividing into stanzas for group work. Prepare class copies of the poem in its entirety as well as copies of individual stanzas for small-group work. We strongly recommend "Alligator Pie."

Introduction to poem and choral reading

Present the poem on overhead, data projector, or chart paper. Ask students to decide whether it is a poem or not and to explain how they know. They must support their decision with clear evidence. Elicit comments on word arrangement (e.g., in stanzas), use of commas at line ends, text shorter than most stories and informational texts, and so on.

Organize students in groups of 4 or 5, distributing one stanza to each group. Brainstorm with students different ways that their stanza could be read; encourage students to add actions that dramatize their stanza. Try to arrange for groups to have space where their practice will not be heard and viewed by other groups. Circulate during group work to ensure that all students are engaged.

Explain to students that the poem should be read as a whole despite the fact that each group has a stanza — they will need to maintain appropriate pacing to do this. Discuss with students how they would like to read their stanza (e.g., shouting, whispering, reading quickly, reading slowly, reading in a choppy way, singing) and what actions they could accompany their reading with. (For example, "Alligator Pie" can involve pretending to shoot with a hockey stick.) Encourage students to practise.

When groups present, remind students to listen and view actively and respectfully, following the pacing established by the first group.

Writing based on a framework

Post the poem in focus in its entirety on chart paper, whiteboard, or SMART Board for student viewing. Tell students that they will be writing a new stanza for the poem.

Discuss with students the poem's layout and similarities among stanzas, patterns, rhyming scheme, and word choices. Use colored highlighters to draw students' attention to the similarities. Help students to see that "Alligator Pie" has a very clear structure. For example, in the first line of each stanza, *Alligator* is paired up with a food — pie, soup, or stew — and this word forms the rhyming scheme for the rest of the stanza.

Sample Student Stanza
Alligator cake, alligator cake
If I don't get some, I think I'm gonna shake.
Give away my turtle, give away my snake,
But don't give away my alligator cake.

With students, create a stanza framework for writing. For example:
Line 1: Alligator [name of food] Alligator [name of food],
Line 2: If I don't get some, I think I'm gonna [action word that rhymes with food from line 1],
Line 3: Give away my [object], give away my [related object that rhymes with food from line 1],
Line 4: But don't give away my Alligator [name of food].

Using shared writing (where students contribute ideas and the teacher ensures that words and phrases are consistent with the structure before recording in writing), create one new stanza for the poem. Chorally read the new stanza as a whole class, ensuring that the rhyme and rhythm of the original poem have been maintained.

Organize students in their groups and distribute a copy of the original poem to each group. Remind them to refer to the posted stanza framework. Reinforce that their task is to write and then chorally read and perform the new stanza much like the large group just modelled. (Endeavor to ensure that each group has space where their practice will not be overheard.) Encourage students to practise so that they will be well prepared to chorally read and perform their new stanza.

Extending the comprehension, appreciation, and response to poetry

Encourage students to try out one or more of the following ideas.
- *Option 1:* Review other poems by the same author — discuss the style of writing. With older students, you might review *So Cool!* by Dennis Lee as it uses his same flare for language but is much more serious than *Alligator Pie* or *Garbage Delight*.
- *Option 2:* Compare the poems of Dennis Lee with those of another contemporary children's poet (e.g., Jack Prelutsky). Ask: "What do the poems have in common? What makes a good children's poem?" Students may tell you that the poem is exciting, has rhythm, and makes them want to join in. They might also say that they like poems because they tend to be short and easy to understand, and when they write them, they don't have to worry about punctuation.
- *Option 3:* Create a class book with the original poem, the new group stanzas, and blank pages. Send the book home, encouraging each family to add and illustrate a new stanza in collaboration with their child.
- *Option 4:* Challenge students to choose a new poem from the anthologies provided in class and to write a new version using their selected poem as a model (scaffold by reminding them of the work they did with "Alligator Pie"). Create a class anthology with the original poem and student creations.

Navigating Found Poetry

Poetry Lesson Plan 2
Selected Texts: *The Whales' Song* by Dyan Sheldon (illustrated by Gary Blythe) and various teacher-selected texts representing a balance of fiction and non-fiction

Found poetry is a natural link to reading since its foundation is in text. Students choose direct quotations, random phrases, or words from a variety of genres, texts, and formats to create an original poem. They manipulate these phrases and words, and piece them together in a novel way that creates a strong and powerful image. Found poetry often provides a scaffolding to poetry writing that allows students to explore literary devices and vocabulary in a non-threatening way. It also actively engages problem-solving and critical thinking as students must review their text source with a specific purpose and message in mind. They do not, however, need to make their text rhyme or impose a particular structure.

Introduction to found poetry

Do a read-aloud (e.g., *The Whales' Song* by Dyan Sheldon). Model by thinking aloud and recording on the board, chart paper, or overhead how to choose words and phrases from the author's text and how to rearrange them into poetic form (see the sample in the margin, next page). Demonstrate repetition, word placement on the page, and how to find rhythmic sections. Show students just enough to get the idea.

Organize students in groups of 4 or 5. Give each student the previously prepared text from the read-aloud, ensuring that the font size and spacing are large

Found in _The Whales' Song_
Whales
    most wondrous creatures
Whales
    as big as the hills
    as peaceful as the moon
Whales
    as large as the mountains
    bluer than the sky
Whales
    moved as if they were dancing
    their voices like the wind
Whales
    enormous in the ocean
    their singing filled up the night
Whales
    most wondrous creatures

enough so that students can easily cut words and phrases apart to rearrange them in poetic form. (Doing this lessens the demand on writing and frees students to play with words.) While students are working in small groups, encourage them to

• observe, offer suggestions, and contribute words, thoughts, and ideas to create a found poem
• independently review the text, highlighting words they consider deliciously poetic
• compare their highlighted sections and come to a consensus of what to use in their found poem
• cut their text into words and phrases, arranging and rearranging, reading and rereading until they have created a poem they can be proud of

Subsequent sessions: Exploring different ways to find poems

Consider doing one or more of the following with your students.

Encounter A: Creating found poems with picture books

Choose a variety of well-written picture books or stories. Organize students in groups of 4 or 5 and provide at least 3 or 4 texts to choose from. Encourage the students in groups to read the texts, first individually, and then together; decide which text will be their source for the found poem by taking turns reading aloud the best selections each has chosen; read aloud the agreed-upon text in its entirety — while one student is reading, the others note words and phrases they like the sound of; scribe or record, while other group members contribute their favorite poetic lines from the text read together; and reread what has been written so far, as others search for themes, adjust the sequencing, identify lines for effective repetition, and finally reach a consensus on the final form.

Encounter B: Using a blackout approach with information texts

Choose a variety of well-written information texts bound by a classroom topic or area of interest (perhaps chapters out of classroom textbooks, Internet website content, newspaper or magazine articles). Organize students in groups of 4 or 5, and provide a range of texts (at least 3 or 4) to choose from. Encourage the students in groups to read the texts, first individually, and then together; reach a consensus about which text will be the source of their found poem and then read aloud the text in its entirety; "black out" words and phrases that they feel are unnecessary while one student reads; and compare what they have blacked out, creating a master copy, chiselling away a word or phrase at a time until they have found their masterpiece.

Encounter C: Creating found poems with environmental text

Create a poem found from your environment. To do so, gather words from around the classroom, ensuring that they are common words students will readily recognize; copy these words onto cue cards or sticky notes that can be rearranged until you have constructed a poem that creates an image or idea.

Explain to students that poems can be found anywhere in our daily experience, if we are open and willing to look. Show students the process you undertook, complete with movable words. Read your found poem, and ask students to contribute more words. Let them see how to take seemingly unconnected words and phrases and rearrange them until a poem is found.

Encourage students to gather poetic words and phrases that they come across as they wander around the school; they can create found poems using the same process outlined in Encounter A.

Beyond found poetry to writing process

No matter which encounter you've selected for the day, encourage students to revise and edit final copies of their poems during writers' workshop. Students' poems can be published in a class anthology. Invite each group to read aloud its poem so that students can compare the final products and recognize that, although they all began with similar texts, the poems are all different. No one poem is more *correct* than another.

Remind students that found poems can be used as summaries of readings, abstracts of projects, and responses to literature. Invite students to keep a writer's notebook in which they gather words and phrases they might describe as "deliciously poetic."

Becoming Poets in Practice and in Action

- Examine preconceived notions towards poetry. Were your experiences positive or negative? What do your students understand about what poetry is and is not?
- Familiarize yourself with as many different types of poems as possible — the purposes for poetry are endless in the classroom.
- Build a love of and respect for poetry by immersing yourself and your students in it — always have a poem in your pocket for that "just right" moment.
- Read aloud poems by different authors; make poetry anthologies available in the classroom.
- Look for the poetry in everyday experiences — find a poem in the schoolyard, in the halls, in a book, or in a movie. Poetry is everywhere!
- Encourage students to write poems in response to what they experience, view, and read.
- Keep the enjoyment in poetry — focus on process and resist the urge to make it all rhyme.
- Be a poet in practice and in action. Challenge yourself a little more as time passes. What poems do you like to write? Where are you comfortable? What can you work towards? Be sure to model and share your practice with your students, no matter how scary!
- Encourage your students to be poets in practice and in action too. Start small, reward their efforts, encourage risk taking, and gradually release responsibility as their confidence grows.
- Introduce new poetic forms; read aloud and display examples of poems that use — or reinvent — the form.
- Create a poetry centre/corner in the classroom where students can read, write, and respond to poetry on an ongoing basis. Create an audit trail of poems encountered in the classroom. Post a list of words that students can arrange and rearrange until they find a poem.
- Have students write their own rhymes and parodies of nursery rhymes or experienced poems; collect them in a classroom anthology available for self-selected reading time and home circulation.

- Choose and use a poem of the week for transition times, for drama, as a model for writing, and for shared reading — send it home each week in a poetry book illustrated by students.
- Infuse poetry into your classroom regularly as opposed to viewing it as a subject to be taught. Let students choose poetry as a viable form of writing.
- Create a low-risk environment in which to share and experience poetry. Writing is a risky venture, so we must be sure to provide positive feedback and encouragement; mentor texts; and lots of modelling and demonstration.
- Build a poetry anchor chart to outline different forms of poetry for student reference. With each addition to the anchor chart, include an example encountered or created in the class. Below is the beginning of a chart.

Selected Poetry Websites
How to write poetry with Jack Prelutsky: http://teacher.scholastic.com/writewit/poetry/jack_my_poem.htm
Performing poetry: www.gigglepoetry.com/
Perform-a-Poem: http://performapoem.lgfl.org.uk/
Writing poetry with J. Patrick Lewis: www.jpatricklewis.com

Kinds of Poetry

A. Acrostic: A poem that uses a single word as an organizational framework. Each line begins with a letter written to the left.
An acrostic poem is easy to write
Can be about any subject
Record each letter of your subject on the left
Organize your words, phrases, and thoughts using these letters
Sentences work well, but so do individual words
Try a combination of both
Imagine your subject as a poem
Create!

B. Bio-poem: A poem written about one's self or a character, including thoughts, feelings, and beliefs. It can be altered to include goals, personality traits, dreams, and ambitions. Each line fulfills a specific purpose.
[*first name*] Frederick
[*four descriptive traits*] Dreamer, Creative, Imaginative, Shy
Sibling of Mice
Lover of Words, Colors, Images
Who feels different from the others
Who needs to contribute positively
Who gives food, color, and stories to his comrades
Who fears ridicule
Who would like to see more of the world
Resident of the wall by the granary
[*Last name or another name*] Poet-Mouse

C. Narrative: Poems that tell a story either in rhyme or unrhymed lines.
'Twas the night before poetry, when all through the school,
Not a student was writing, not even those cool!
The stories were told to each other with care,
In hopes narrative poems soon would be there. . . .

D. Free verse: Poetry written in either rhymed or unrhymed lines that have no set pattern.
Snow
As fresh as a spring day,
As cold as ice,
As wet as water,
Like a soft, white blanket,
Quieter than a sleeping village,
Fresh, cold, wet, soft, quiet
Snow.

Freeing Children to Focus on Words and Sounds

Characteristics that distinguish effective readers from readers "at risk" and ultimately, effective writers from writers "at risk" include awareness of rhyme, rhythm, and alliteration and *phonemic* awareness (the ability to hear, say, and manipulate sounds in words). The sad fact that some children enter school without the benefit of these rich language experiences makes it all the more imperative that these opportunities are provided throughout the school day. While not all children require phonemic awareness activities, some can benefit from more intensive attention to the letters and sounds of the English language.

Poetry provides a natural opportunity to play with language and reinforce these needs in a small-group or mini-lesson setting. Repeated readings of poetry can provide opportunities for students to focus on one-to-one word correspondence as well as attending to word patterns and word families. For these children, daily reading of poetry through personal poetry books would be beneficial both at home and at school.

Routman (2000) challenges us to consider the freedom students often feel with poetry. Students who typically struggle with writing letters, words, and sentences, often finding writing burdensome, blossom in this genre. Poetry frees them from restrictions due to content, form, space, length, conventions, and rhyme; with poetry, they can let their imaginations soar.

The following poem illustrates the freedom that students can find in poetry. It was written by a group of five Grade 3–4 students who received daily resource support in reading and writing. After reading many spooky tales and poems over a two-week period, they composed this poem, rehearsed it, and performed it during morning announcements over the public address system.

A Spooky Poem

In a cave
Bats at night,
Dragon sleeping,
Ghosts at night.

Child missing,
People looking,
Wolf howling
At the moon.

Spiders creeping,
Ogres shrieking,
In the night,
In the night.
— Brittany, Chrissy, Shawna, George, and Christine

Assessing Read, Written, and Presented Poetry

Assessment of poetry is deemed by many to be tricky. This belief often results from a fear of passing judgment on a child's creative work or from lack of confidence and familiarity with poetry writing. Effective assessment of poetry always focuses on growth and moving the student along the continuum of poetry writing. It is important to focus on the expectations established with students, poetic structures taught, and the processes for poetry writing established in the classroom. Be sure to observe throughout a term rather than to base assessment on one or two poems.

When assessing poetry reading, do not concentrate overly on analysis. Most students dread this and many teachers resist poetry reading and writing in the classroom because of this. Instead, focus on whether students

- understand the difference between poetry and prose and identify unique features of poetry
- offer meanings, interpretations, and personal reactions to poems
- make a variety of connections between poems, other texts, and everyday life
- apply comprehension strategies previously taught (For example: Can they make predictions, inferences, and draw conclusions?)
- identify some poetic devices used by poets (e.g., metaphor, simile, alliteration, rhyme, rhythm, repetition)

When assessing poetry writing, observe to see whether students

- use language in playful ways to create a variety of poetic forms
- identify and apply poetic structures taught in the classroom (For example: Can they follow the structure of an acrostic or bio-poem? Can they evoke an image through a free-verse poem?)
- follow established models to create new poems (For example: Can they use an existing poem to write a new one?)
- demonstrate a visual or conceptual awareness of the poetic through the physical arrangement of words, phrases, lines, spacing, punctuation, indentation, and so on
- identify deliciously poetic words and phrases and use resources to find appropriate vocabulary
- include some poetic devices in their writing
- read aloud their own poetry to check its effect and revise as necessary

When assessing the presentation or performance of poetry (or talk about it), observe to see whether students

- use their voices appropriately to convey meaning, interpretation, mood, and intent
- experiment with pitch, pause, and pace to improve choral presentations
- investigate possibilities of using voice, sound, and movement to enhance choral presentations
- follow directions, offer advice, and contribute ideas to the choral presentation
- have an appropriate sense of audience as audience members and as performers

More Strategies for Engaging Students in Poetry

Keep a poem in your pocket. Share the poem at just the right moment — or plan to have poetry breaks at different times during the day; encourage your students to do the same thing. Be sure to choose poems that are easy to remember (or copy text onto a cue card).

Initiate, organize, and support school-wide celebrations of poetry. On a selected day, create a school newsletter, read aloud poems over the public address system, try to arrange for children's poets to visit the school, conduct poetry work-

Poem in My Pocket: Excerpt
I've a poem in my pocket
But no one needs to know
I can hide it, I can lock it
Or I can share it, make it grow.

I've a poem in my head
To my fingers, let it flow
I can write it, make it said
If I share it, it will grow. . . .
— Michelann Parr

shops, and create a school anthology of poems. Have an assembly that highlights poetry written in the school — begin with a teacher performance of a favorite poem. Create a school poem, where each class contributes a line, or develop a class poem that grows as each student adds a line or a stanza. (Georgia Heard's *Falling Down the Page: A Book of List Poems* is a great model to use for this.)

Create class poetry anthologies. These can be either teacher created, which is particularly effective with younger students, or student created. The anthologies can be collections of poems written by students in the classroom or they can be compilations of poems collected and selected for a specific purpose. Older students can review published poetry anthologies with the intent of creating their own. Discussion points include theme, selection of poems, organization, illustration, and presentation. (For further information, see www.poetryclass.net/Dymoke002.pdf.)

Open up a poetry centre. A poetry centre allows students to explore, respond to, and extend poems introduced and discussed through read-aloud or shared/choral reading. Look for poems that are exciting and represent a wide variety of topics. When selecting poems, think about your students' interests and what they can relate to. At a centre, students might put a poem back together using a pocket chart; illustrate a poem; write a new stanza; record a poem; set the poem to music; compare two poems; make new poems by manipulating magnetic words; and review poetry anthologies to find similar poems.

Pair poetry with art. Use Sarah L. Thomson's *Imagine a Day*, David Booth's *Images of Nature*, or David Bouchard's *The Elders Are Watching* as mentor texts to demonstrate how visual art can be paired with poetry. Collect visual images from calendars; model how to write a free-verse poem based on a picture. Provide a wide variety of pictures and poetry anthologies; match existing poems to the pictures. Students then write their own.

Prompt students to produce poetry videos or digital poetry. Poetry videos challenge students "to find the perfect poem" or perhaps one they've written and mix its lyrics with visual images, movement, and/or music (tapping into multiple ways of being). Students can explore the connections between music lyrics and poems, keeping in mind that songs are poems put to music and that not all poems rhyme. Poetry videos might also take the form of digital poems that make use of PowerPoint or Keynote. In this instance, the text of the poem is presented on screen in addition to being read.

Inviting Families to Share Poems

- Nursery rhymes and finger plays are often first heard in the home. For younger children, send home an invitation to parents to send in their child's favorites so that you can make connections between home and school. Create a "travelling" class anthology of family rhymes. Encourage multilingual families to send rhymes in two languages, particularly if the child has learned the rhyme in both languages or in a language other than English.
- If, like many teachers, you have each student maintain an anthology of poems studied within class, send home this anthology on a regular basis to be shared with families. Encourage families to chant with their children and explore different ways of reading a poem (e.g., in different voices, loudly, whisper-read).

"Poetry is the record of the best and happiest moments of the happiest and best minds."
— Percy Bysshe Shelley

For further information, see www.educationoasis.com/resources/Articles/creating_poetry_videos.htm and www.unf.edu/~nstanley/powerpoint.htm.

- Make use of popular songs and ballads. Invite students to talk to their parents about songs of their generation; they can compare current popular songs with those of their parents' generation.
- Ask the parents of your students to send in titles of poems they remember from childhood. Surprise them by sending home a full text of the poem with some suggestions for sharing it with their child. You might ask: *Why do you remember this poem? What does it make you think about? Did it make you laugh, smile, cry, or sigh?*

Literacy Essential 8: Children need poetry! Use poetry, with all its oral appeal and liberating potential, to engage students in playing with and exploring language, both aloud and written.

Poetry Texts for Children

Depending on the purpose, poems can be used for any grade level so we hesitate to level them here.

Single-authored works

If You're Not Here, Please Raise Your Hand: Poems About School by Kalli Dakos
Creatures of Earth, Sea, and Sky: Poems by Georgia Heard
Alligator Pie by Dennis Lee
The Canadian Railroad Trilogy by Gordon Lightfoot (Art by Ian Wallace)
Hey World, Here I Am! by Jean Little
Where the Sidewalk Ends by Shel Silverstein
Seasons by Aska Warabé
Color Me a Rhyme: Nature Poems for Young People by Jane Yolen
Beyond the Great Mountains: A Visual Poem About China by Ed Young
A World of Wonders: Geographic Travels in Verse and Rhyme by J. Patrick Lewis

Edited anthologies

'Til All the Stars Have Fallen edited by David Booth
Falling Down the Page: A Book of List Poems edited by Georgia Heard
A Foot in the Mouth: Poems to Speak, Sing, and Shout edited by Paul J. Janeczko
Talking to the Sun: An Illustrated Anthology of Poems for Young People edited by Kenneth Koch and Kate Farrell
This Same Sky: A Collection of Poems from Around the World edited by Naomi Shihab Nye
The Random House Book of Poetry for Children edited by Jack Prelutsky
Sing a Song of Popcorn: Every Child's Book of Poems edited by Beatrice Schenk de Regniers, Eva Moore, Mary Michaels White, and Jan Carr
Imaginary Gardens: American Poetry and Art for Young People edited by Charles Sullivan

CHAPTER 9

A Dynamic Way of Knowing: Drama

> I believe that every child I meet understands deep, basic matters worthy of exploration but they may as yet have no language for them. One of the languages they may develop is through dramatic work.
>
> — Dorothy Heathcote

Drama and play are intimately connected. Dramatic play emerges in childhood long before children enter school; we see little ones exploring meaningful everyday events through make-believe play or pretending to be something they're not in an effort to understand and make sense of their own identities and realities, and perhaps rehearse a little for later life. In their play, they can be great hockey players, dancers, construction workers, letter carriers, talk-show hosts, mommies, daddies, and teachers.

Drama enables students to interact in different ways with others, develop social skills, and build community; students explore roles, perspectives, and values that are different than their own, both to understand and rehearse. Drama develops such skills as creativity, enquiry, communication, empathy, cooperation, problem-solving, decision-making, negotiation, and leadership, that can, in turn, be applied in various contexts and learning situations.

Drama as Participation

Drama, to us, is participation. It is a process that over days, multiple encounters, and rehearsals and revisions *may* end in performance, but not always.

Because drama is participation, it is critical to recognize that not all students, or teachers, will have the same comfort level entering drama. So teachers need to model and engage, stressing that "We're all in this together, and I will never ask you to do something that I'm not willing to do myself."

There are various ways to ensure that your classroom allows students to participate within their comfort zones. Involve students in the selection of activities and the negotiation of success criteria. Change the goals of activities for individual students, ensuring that they meet with success, gradually increasing the expectations as their comfort level develops. At times, this might mean limiting the number of required activities, the level of participation, or shortening up the time to complete activities. Some students will benefit from limited and defined spaces for drama. (For example: Can they do the activity at their desk, on the

Drama as a Form of Expression
"In the past, I had thought about drama as being about the performance, as when my children would learn their parts for the Christmas pantomime. Now I understand drama . . . to be about teaching students to express themselves, to communicate, to enhance comprehension, and foster oral language development. Drama can be a way to engage students who may be having difficulty with the written language; a way to express themselves through their bodies or their voices."
— Rosemary Sidorko, classroom teacher

reading carpet, or in a hula hoop?) As always, plan opportunities to model, provide explicit instruction, and participate.

Drama appeals to learners on many different levels. Some will be far more comfortable preparing scripts and props or dramatizing in small groups; others seem to be born actors, comfortable with improvising in front of the class. Consider such differences when planning activities, and ensure that there are many levels of involvement and engagement possible.

We recommend approaching drama lessons or workshops in the same way we envision conducting a physical education lesson.

- *Start with a warm-up.* Enter drama with tasks designed to make participants feel comfortable. The purpose is to get them moving and active, exploring, experimenting, taking risks, focusing, and concentrating. Quick activities ease students into drama in much the same way a warm-up precedes a workout.
- *Prepare for active engagement.* This phase is dependent on the purpose established by the teacher.

> Story drama encourages students to go beyond traditional comprehension to an exploration of roles and perspectives offered.
>
> Content drama is organized in a way that allows students to learn, practise, and review content in an active and practical way.
>
> Drama for community building brings together a variety of activities that allow students to interact, problem-solve, and gain an understanding of self and peers.
>
> Drama for problem solving presents students with tasks that require them to communicate, negotiate, and find creative solutions.

- *Provide a cool down.* There is a voluntary sharing of drama as experienced and practised during active engagement. As the lesson or workshop comes to a close, there should also be debriefing, self-assessment, and reflection on the task and learning.

Using Drama to Scaffold Expression of Learning

A holistic drama approach allows students to explore story and content in oral, interpersonal, and low-risk ways — students get so involved in the fun and action that there is less focus on the story/content. That, however, truly drives the drama. Drama becomes an integral part of the processes of reading response and transactional writing; it serves as scaffolding to the independent expression of students' learning in other formats.

Warm-up

- Set a purpose for listening. In the case of *Rainbow Crow*, read the author's note aloud. Ask students to listen to determine the Lenape legend being told (why the crow looks and sounds like it does). Alternatively, use the story to introduce social studies units on topics such as community and interdependence; science units on seasons or animal groups; visual arts units on mixed media and illustration; music and movement units on rhythm; and literature–social studies units on legends.
- Read aloud *Rainbow Crow*.

Drama Lesson Plan 1

Selected Text: *Rainbow Crow* by Nancy Van Laan

Rainbow Crow is a text rich in story and legend of how things on earth came to be. It describes how Spring came to the land, breaking the pattern of ever-deepening snow.

- Discuss characters. Ask: "Who are the characters? What do we know about them? How do we know this?"
- Let students warm up with appropriate and relevant activities, such as these:

> *Voice:* Chant lines from the story: "Aiya, aiya, aiya, aiya, / Rain, Rainbow Crow, / Stop the snow, Crow . . ."
>
> *Movement:* Use hands and simple movements to move like some of the animals before and after the snowfall.
>
> *Tableaux:* Have small groups capture their interpretation of the beginning, middle, and ending of the story. (A sample anchor chart is shown below.)

Tableaux

A tableau is a frozen action shot or picture created using only your bodies. There are no props and typically, no speaking, unless a narrator is assigned.

- Choose at least one significant moment from a text that you would like to share or portray.
- Discuss how you would like to present these moments or scenes to the rest of the class.
- Create a scene, with all members participating. Think of what we see in pictures: objects may be high or low; people may be looking in different directions or at the camera.
- Freeze each scene for approximately 10 seconds (just like we would to take a picture), then flow seamlessly into the next scene.
- Two to three scenes are usually presented to capture the essence of the text or story.
- Choose one cue — a clap, a stomp, a word — to signal your transition from one scene to the next.

Active engagement

Ask the class to divide into groups, and assign each group a drama task (which will take 30 to 45 minutes). Ensure that each task has a task card reminding students of what they need to know and any information they need access to in order to complete the drama. Ideally, every student will have the opportunity to explore all tasks using a rotation system. (Exploring all tasks will prepare them to engage in all of the post-drama activities.)

- Group 1 composes, rehearses, and performs a readers theatre script that summarizes the Lenape legend and the journey of Rainbow Crow. Remind students to use snippets of dialogue and narration from the book to prepare their script. Challenge them to carry their summary with dialogue rather than relying heavily on narration; if necessary, suggest that they recast some of the narration as dialogue. For example, *So he asked the Great Spirit to stop the snow* could be spoken by Rainbow Crow as, "Great Spirit, please stop the snow."

> **Readers Theatre**
> Readers theatre is the reading of a text with others in front of an audience.
> The text might be from a story you've read or content you'd like to share in an alternative format. In readers theatre, a small group prepares and performs a script, usually with one or two narrators and several characters.

"The learning in drama is like a voice saying: 'This is what life is like; this is how people are; this is the way that human encounters work.'"
— David Booth and Charles Lundy (1985, pp. ix–x)

111

1. Brainstorm ideas for scripts and make a decision.
2. Reread your selected text carefully, highlighting or noting lines you'd like to use or adapt in your script.
3. Determine how many characters and narrators you need. Even in content scripts, you need to have characters!
4. Create a script, with all members participating. Make sure that everyone has a set of colored cue cards or sticky notes so that you can each write your lines down and then rearrange until your ideal script is found.
5. Revise, edit, and polish your script; ensure that everyone has a copy.
6. Rehearse your script, paying attention to how your voices are used to bring characters to life and show how they feel, who they are, or how they fit in with the story. When rehearsing, focus on developing fluency, speed, volume, and expression.

Remember: In readers theatre, there are few, if any special effects, scenery, costumes, or music and no memorization of lines.

- Group 2 chooses one of these scenarios to address: (a) What might have happened if a different animal had gone in search of a way to stop the snow? (b) How might the animals have dealt with the deepening snow as they awaited Rainbow Crow's return? The group composes a brief, written script, practises it, and performs the play.
- Group 3 improvises a conversation that might take place between Black Crow and some of the animals long after his return to the forest with fire; conversations can be planned and recorded through a graphic organizer.
- Group 4 collaboratively designs and presents a monologue on Black Crow's behalf, expressing his inner thoughts and feelings about losing his beautiful voice and colored feathers (see Chapter 6 for an example of the subtext strategy and making inner thoughts visible). Encourage students to think about oral expression, movement, and gestures that will enhance the monologue. Groups should record speaking notes in written form.

Cool down

Students choose one multi-level, independent writing activity, such as these:
- In role as an animal glad that the snow has melted, create a thank-you card to Black Crow, as he became, outlining what you are thankful for.
- Write a journal entry about Rainbow Crow's journey to find fire and his feelings on the journey.
- Write a letter from the Great Spirit to Black Crow. Exchange letters with a classmate and write the crow's response.
- Write a legend about a different animal in the story (perhaps why the moose has antlers).

All students can then participate in guided reflection on the drama process, using success criteria such as these:

Success Criteria for Drama

As you work with your group, think about these assessment and success criteria:

"A broad definition of educational drama is 'role-taking' either to understand a social situation more thoroughly or to experience imaginatively via identification in social situations . . . Dramatic activity is the direct result of the ability to role play — to want to know how it feels to be in someone else's shoes."
— Dorothy Heathcote (1984, p. 49)

Group:

☐ We focus our attention on the task.

☐ We gather and prepare required resources efficiently and effectively.

☐ We work within established time guidelines and use our time well.

☐ We manage space and movement, keeping safety and respect in mind.

☐ We collaborate well in creating the drama.

☐ We take turns during discussions.

☐ We work as a group and present one continuous drama.

☐ We focus and stay in role throughout the drama.

Self:

☐ I focus my attention on the task right away.

☐ I collaborate in a variety of situations.

☐ I take turns during discussions.

☐ I accept different points of view and build on the ideas of others.

☐ I follow along and listen attentively during rehearsals, contributing my parts at the right time.

☐ I offer suggestions to help my group revise and shape ideas for presentation (e.g., deciding what to include, how lines should be read, how to move throughout the drama).

Navigating Content Through Drama to Non-traditional Responses

Drama Lesson Plan 2
Selected Text: "Twas the Night" in *Science Verse* by Jon Scieszka

Jon Scieszka's books are excellent to use as springboards for content drama. His poems draw together poetry and facts in a way that entertains, but also instructs. Kicking off a workshop or theme with a poem energizes students, makes them want to learn more, and provides them with a model to use in their own content writing.

This lesson also draws on a range of fiction and non-fiction titles on the theme of space.

The following section provides a demonstration of how drama can be used as a means of learning curriculum content, in this case, scientific content on space. It demonstrates our multiple ways of knowing approach to literacy and the integration of drama with studies in the content areas. This approach enhances student engagement, reduces the possibility of regurgitation and plagiarism, and strengthens the connection between what students know and what they need to learn.

The workshop involves *aesthetic* reading, or reading for pure enjoyment — for example, a poem — and *efferent* reading, which is for real-world purposes. In efferent reading, attention is focused on information that is to be extracted or retained from the text. Every text can be read from both an efferent and an aesthetic stance that is a reflection of the reader's orientation, intention, or purpose for reading.

Warm up

- Chorally read a theme-related poem or short text.
- Use an anticipation guide to find out what students know and don't know about the chosen topic (e.g., Space Fact or Fib), and to stimulate the desire to find out

more (see Chapter 6, page 80). For example, for "Space Fact or Fib," distribute paper stars, each with a statement about aspects of space. Have students read the statements aloud and predict which represent facts and which, fibs. For example:

> The Northern Lights, or aurora borealis, were once thought to be dead souls trying to tell the living that summer will return. (Fact: Saami people of Arctic Europe)

> When you see the Northern Lights, if you whistle, they will jump closer and make a crackling sound. (Fib)

- Challenge students during their readings and activities to find information that either supports or refutes their assessment of fact or fib.
- Divide the class into three groups: comet experts, planet experts, and astronaut experts. Explain to students that they will be gathering information on their designated theme and designing a dramatic presentation that will present their information to the class; emphasize that all students must be involved in the drama. (A number of student dramas are outlined under Active engagement.)

Active engagement

Ensure that all presentations are recorded, edited, and made available on the classroom computer.

Students brainstorm different ways that they can present information (e.g., a trivia game, a game show, a fashion show, a news report, a play, readers theatre). Record all responses for student reference. Emphasize that they must present content in a fun, energizing, and educational way. They have to make their audience remember the facts that they choose to present. Alternatively, students requiring high levels of guidance and support could be assigned tasks similar to the ones presented below.

Once the brainstorming is complete, divide students into groups of 4 to 6. Allow each group time to decide upon the type of presentation as well as the content of the presentation. As a teacher, ensure that each group's presentation style and content are different. Plan for 45 to 60 minutes for initial rehearsal, and then encourage students to take time during literacy workshop to rehearse. Remind them that only final presentations will be recorded; this will free them up to focus on process and learning of content.

Here are a few presentation ideas:

Group 1: Cometrivia! Students use props (an assortment of rings, hula hoops, Nerf balls, smooshie balls, ribbons) to present the information they gather in concrete ways. They design information cards and read them as part of the presentation.

Sample comet information for cards:

> Comets get their name from the Greek word "kometes," which means "long hair," a reference to their long tails.

> Jets of gas and dust form long tails that we can see from earth. These tails can sometimes be millions of miles long.

> Comets orbit the sun, but have such a big orbit it takes some comets millions of years to orbit.

> When earth passes through the tail of a comet, we see meteor showers.

Group 2: PlanetExtravaganza! Students gather information and prepare five important details about each planet. They decide on a presentation format to dramatize their information. For example, they might present a fashion show, where each student is a planet and walks the runway in role as suggested by the accompanying script, for example: "Saturn is adorned with multiple rings that surround her being. As she spins down the runway, observe how her rings . . ." The fashion show might begin with a description of the term *planet*, as can be found on the NASA website (http://missionscience.nasa.gov/nasascience/what_is_aplanet.html):

What is a planet?

Technically, there was never a scientific definition of the term Planet before 2006. When the Greeks observed the sky thousands of years ago, they discovered objects that acted differently than stars. These points of light seemed to wander around the sky throughout the year. We get the term "planet" from the Greek word "Planetes" — meaning wanderer . . .

Group 3: Astroviews Students begin their work by considering this question: "Do astronauts see stars when they are in space?" They can then go on to a full exploration of what astronauts see and do not see when they are orbiting the earth. Students can present their findings as a panel discussion that involves a number of astronauts who give descriptions and sketches of what they saw in space. The drama could be presented as a timeline beginning with the first time an astronaut was on the moon through to what today's astronauts see in space.

Cool down

Here are a variety of non-traditional ways for students to extend the learning gained from the drama-related activities:

- Write a newspaper report about an aspect of the solar system using the 5 Ws + H (who, what, when, where, why, and how)
- View videos that relate to space exploration (e.g., BBC *The Planets* and *Space*; multiple video clips at www.space.com; or *Universe* at www.nfb.ca/film/Universe/)
- Write a song or poem, or develop a webquest (Internet treasure hunt) or media presentation about space.
- Participate in a virtual field trip to space, using simulations on various websites (e.g., NASA Kids Club: www.nasa.gov/audience/forkids/kidsclub/flash/index.html; NASA Solar System Exploration: http://solarsystem.nasa.gov/kids/index.cfm; BBC Space: www.bbc.co.uk/science/space/; National Geographic Space: http://science.nationalgeographic.com/science/space/)
- Using facts from the NASA website, write an acrostic poem using a space word or develop a found poem.

Applying Drama Skills to Life

Assessment should always be about enhancing participation and comfort level, or risk-taking.

"In pretend play, children use language and thinking skills to compare, plan, investigate materials, problem solve, experiment, negotiate, and evaluate. Engaging in pretend play also supports children's development of self-regulation and subsequently strengthens their ability to learn through engaging with people and resources in their environment." (Ontario Ministry of Education, 2010–11, p. 70)

It is important that expectations are clearly described and that the processes (not just a final product or performance) are carefully observed. Assessment criteria apply to the process and to performance. Process criteria can include collaborative skills. Performance criteria can include use of voice and movement, expression, and fluency. As with all meaningful assessment, the ultimate purpose of assessment is to inform future teaching and provide feedback to students that will encourage growth.

The list of questions below is designed with those principles in mind. You may adopt any of them and have students use them for self-assessment.

Questions to Promote Reflection on Drama

- Did you feel most comfortable working with a partner, in a small group, or with the whole class? Why?
- What dramatic activities are you most comfortable with? Why?
- Write down three things you learned about yourself through drama.
- What skills does a person need to develop to take part and be comfortable in drama?
- How much of yourself did you find in the roles you played?

A way to assess other literacy domains

In addition, teacher assessment of drama activities can be used to assess other domains of literacy, such as reading comprehension. As an alternative to written responses to teacher-posed questions, dramatic responses can demonstrate deeper, individualized understandings of texts. This can be especially beneficial for English Language Learners and those students who struggle with the mechanics of reading and writing, but who may display strengths in the use of movement and voice.

Managing the Classroom for Drama

- Establish consistent signals. Oral cues might be "Lights, camera, action" or "Freeze." Or, you could use a bell or a drum or sticks with different beats for GO and STOP. Have the class practise responding to the cues before engaging in drama activities.
- Use varied spaces for drama. Limit and define the space for drama in order to support students as they explore concepts related to personal space and acceptable distance from others (e.g., at a desk, on the reading carpet, in a hula hoop).
- Provide more teacher modelling and demonstration. For example, use character voices when reading, start off with narrative mime, or participate in the drama yourself. Remember: we should never ask students to do something we are unwilling to do ourselves.
- Provide more teacher guidance for students who require individual coaching. For example, you might ask: "What would happen if you said it this way . . . [moved this way . . .]?"
- Draw on familiar stories or on students' own experiences, including class field trips, for drama activities.

- Make strategic use of visual aids. Use name tags, headbands for individual student use, and minor costuming to help students understand the roles. Masks or simple props such as a microphone can not only pull students into role, but also help them sustain a role longer.
- Keep the levels of difficulty of various drama activities in mind. Mime is easier than verbal improvisation, and individual drama activities directed by the teacher are easier than group work. Gradually increase both as students demonstrate comfort with the activities. Check the conceptual difficulty of the material. If students act silly, it may be that they don't know what to do or feel that they can't do what is expected. Humor and silliness often mask embarrassment. Alter the conceptual difficulty of the material. Gradually increase as students demonstrate increasing competence.
- Be attuned to the specific needs and challenges of your students. Children with hearing impairments need to see your face and mouth; students with English Language Learning needs may need to "echo" their lines, have non-speaking parts, or speak with a partner or in a small group. Ask the students what they can do to help themselves. Don't force shy children to take part — this may increase their reluctance. Instead, set some goals with them, allowing them to enter the drama step by step. If students seem unable to end a drama, provide a specific ending that you thought of earlier, ask the audience for ideas, or take a role and end it ("and then I woke up!").
- Be ready to revise your expectations. Alter what you expect in the conclusion. For example, you may have planned for students to present small-group work to the whole group, but perhaps the group work didn't "work" (or didn't yet). Or, perhaps presentations could be done for just one other group.

More Strategies for Opening Up Drama's Potential

Drama at Home
- Send home scripts, including minimal scripts, after students have practised and presented them in class. Invite family members and caregivers to try them out at home.
- Emphasize that drama is an everyday form of learning — not just the big school musical. Invite family and caregivers to view "everyday drama," such as outlined in this chapter. Have the students write home about the drama activities they have enjoyed that week.

Prompt students to open up their imaginations through objects. One way to do this is to read *Not a Box* or *Not a Stick* by Antoinette Portis, where the character demonstrates how a box or a stick can be so many other things if we open our imaginations. Divide the class into small groups, and give each group an everyday article, perhaps a comb, a skipping rope, a scarf, a rock, or a set of beads. Within each group, students pass around the article, sharing what they imagine the article to be, miming the article's use as they share its purpose. When you select an object for the activity, make sure that you can envision multiple imaginative or real purposes for it.

Explore minimal scripts. Have students work with a partner and practise a four-line script, saying it in different styles, intonations, and expressions. Students can take the lines from the perspective of different characters. They will come to appreciate that it's not what they say, but how they say something that matters.

As Larry Swartz writes in *The New Dramathemes*, ways that students can experiment saying the lines include whispering, as though talking on a telephone, quickly, singing, or with one person saying the lines angrily and the other, calmly. Students can create their own four-line scripts and act them out in different ways.

Engage students in improvisation activities, using a range of approaches.
- Create and use situation improv cards. These are index cards that identify characters and provide simple directions. For example, a scene requires three

characters: a parent, a shop assistant, and a spoiled child. The child wants something he/she cannot have. Students can create their own improv cards too.

- Hot-seat a character from a well-known story (e.g., "The Three Little Pigs"). One student assumes the role of a character and classmates or group members interview the character to find out more about his or her feelings, background, and so on.
- Play Professor Know-It-All. Three students become the talking heads of a professor. The class asks a question, and each of the heads adds a word at a time to create an answer. For example, the class might ask: "Where does fire come from?" The three students, in turn, might respond:

    Fire comes from the Great Spirit in the sky.

- Prompt "Quick Change" emotions. Call out emotions, one at a time, and have students portray a variety of them. (For example: Show me *mad*. Show me *sad*. Show me *surprised*. Show me *jealous*. Show me *silly*.) Students can also be encouraged to freeze at times, unfreezing their eyes to look around and see how their classmates respond. Considering introducing or following up this activity with a reading of *The Way I Feel* by Janan Cain.

Explore miming. Have students act out verbs (and thereby fully understand what they are). For example, ask them to climb stairs, try to whistle, walk on the moon, walk like a queen or king, wave, cut a ribbon, read a speech, put up an umbrella, walk in the rain, stagger in the wind, and twirl the umbrella.

Arrange for students to make "noiseless sounds," where they stand in one place facing one another in small groups. For example, they might mime the following sounds without any noise: a laugh, applause, choking, a sneeze, yawning.

> **Literacy Essential 9:** As a dynamic form of learning, drama belongs squarely in the classroom. When you infuse role-taking and drama strategies into your teaching, student engagement deepens, and you can better bring stories and information to life. Diverse students can use drama as scaffolding to develop further as readers and writers.

Tale, Legend, and Poem Texts for Drama

Stories suitable for story and content drama allow many different levels of student exploration and response that includes, but is not limited to, empathizing with and understanding characters, comparing legend to scientific truths, and researching information to extend understanding of content. The texts below are good alternatives to *Rainbow Crow* by Nancy Van Laan, featured in "Using Drama to Scaffold Expression of Learning," earlier in this chapter.

- *Bringing the Rain to Kapiti Plain* by Verna Aardema
- *The Name of the Tree* by Celia Barker Lottridge
- *A Promise to the Sun: An African Tale* by Tololwa M. Mollel
- *Knots on a Counting Rope* by Bill Martin, Jr.
- *SkySisters* by Jan Bourdeau Waboose
- *Solomon's Tree* by Andrea Spalding
- *The Gift of the Inukshuk* by Mike Ulmer
- *The Wolf of Gubbio* by Michael Bedard
- *The Trial of the Stone* by Richardo Keens-Douglas

These texts are all books of poetry based on content that students may encounter in their studies of math, science, geography, and nature. They lend themselves to dramatic activities, as outlined in "Navigating Content Through Drama to Nontraditional Responses," earlier in this chapter.

- *Math Curse* by Jon Scieszka
- *A World of Wonders: Geographic Travels in Verse and Rhyme* by J. Patrick Lewis
- *The World's Greatest: Poems* by J. Patrick Lewis
- *Monumental Verses* by J. Patrick Lewis
- *Where in the Wild? Camouflaged Creatures Concealed . . . and Revealed* by David Schwartz and Yael Schy
- *All the Wild Wonders: Poems of Our Earth* compiled by Wendy Cooling and Piet Grobler
- *Let's Celebrate!: Festival Poems from Around the World* edited by Debjani Chatterjee and Brian D'Arcy
- *Creatures of Earth, Sea, and Sky: Poems* by Georgia Heard
- *Color Me a Rhyme: Nature Poems for Young People* by Jane Yolen

See also the poetry anthologies listed in Chapter 8.

CHAPTER 10

Acts of Co-creation: Storytelling

I love seeing the look on other people's faces when they hear my story. I like getting help from my friends. It helps make the story better.
— Jaimee, age 10

Storytelling in its traditional form is a distinctive art — the art of using the spoken word and perhaps music, physical movement, and gesture to communicate a story to a live audience. A vital, unique aspect of storytelling is its reliance on the audience to develop their own visual images in order to co-create the story with the storyteller. In this chapter, we look at storytelling both in its traditional oral and 21st century digital forms.

"School life is full of all sorts of contexts for story-making," affirm David Booth and Bob Barton (2000, p. 29). In the classroom, the halls, and the schoolyard, children engage in storytelling and story listening daily. They come to school with stories from home, with ideas about last night's television show, a movie on the weekend, or a new video game. They pass on rumors and retell news stories. When teachers share personal stories about something as simple as taking a dog for a walk in a new park the children listen with rapt attention. When we listen to their stories, we honor who they are and help them find their voices.

Storytelling provides students with opportunities to explore the nature of stories and to develop as story makers. They can experiment with the literary tradition, retelling stories from both traditional and modern sources. They can come to identify the basic shape of a story. They can recall stories and gain understanding of their elements, such as problem, plot, and setting. Through storytelling, they can learn to create characters and dialogue. Given an opportunity to tell stories, they are able to practise oral language skills, such as vocal expression and emphasis. They might discover they have a story when they thought they did not and like the opportunity to share personal stories. They could rehearse stories orally to find their writing voice and to receive feedback before and during writing. In the classroom community, they can celebrate their stories.

Traditional Storytelling in a Workshop Setting

A teacher's modelling is the most potent way of introducing storytelling to students. Tell a story — whether it's a personal anecdote, a published retelling of something from folklore, a true story, or a visual/digital story. A willingness to share your own stories is valuable. A sample experience follows.

The Most Foolish Thing I've Ever Done: Terry Campbell

I have told this story to Grades 4 and 5 students, and to teacher candidates. It always seems to inspire the listeners. After I finish, listeners are directed to form groups for telling their own foolish tales. The only instructions are to take turns listening and telling, to tell a true story, and to stick to the posted time limit (one or two minutes each in a group of six works well). The best thing about this activity is the laughter that fills the whole classroom as students listen to and tell their own tales.

I grew up in a family of six children in Niagara Falls. Two of my brothers, one sister, and I often packed a lunch and embarked on all-day hikes exploring the forests and glens of the gorgeous Niagara landscapes. Our favorite was the Niagara Glen park, set in the escarpment of the lower Niagara River. On one of these treks, when I was about nine years old, the four of us had made our way down to the rocks at the river's edge. At this point, just below the whirlpool, the mighty Niagara River is compressed into a narrow channel — deep, churning, and dangerous. My brother dared us to a game of jumping from rock to rock. I followed him from the shoreline rocks over a gap of green river rapids and onto a flat rock partway out into the river. He blithely bounded back, taunting me to follow. Then I saw where I was. I froze. I looked at the water and at the small party on shore, and said, "I can't get back!" My legs were trembling. My younger sister started to cry. It was that sound that spurred me on to gather myself and make the leap. To this day, if anyone says to me, "Dare ya!" I dig my heels in and refuse to budge.

"Tales are meant to be told. . . . Storytelling, that oldest of arts, has always been both an entertainment and a cultural necessity. Laws, news, customs, even royal successions encapsulated within the bodies of tales were passed on and on, down through the years. As the stories were kept alive by this process of mouth-to-mouth resuscitation, the storytellers breathed life into human cultures."
— Jane Yolen

This workshop involves visualization and collaborative strategies for small-group and partner work. If students are unfamiliar with these, teach or re-teach them before the workshop or on the spot.

Managing movement and voice levels in a storytelling workshop is, of course, important. For a workshop focused on storytelling and story writing, Grade 3 teacher Michelle Hlusek addressed the matter by starting a chart of expectations with the whole group and then leaving the list on the chart stand for a week. Students were invited to add to it. They came up with the following ideas, the italicized type showing the additions:

> Use quiet voices.
> Sit side-by-side or in a small circle when talking or rehearsing.
> Use one of the writing centres for your own writing.
> Keep all your writing together in your Writer's Notebook.
> *Don't talk to me when I am writing!*
> *Put the picture books back after you use them!*

This model workshop engages the learners in a literature-based unit integrating the six language arts with drama, storytelling, poetry, music, movement, and visual art. The storytelling and story listening with selected follow-up activities can be treated as a single lesson and completed in an afternoon. If all suggested activities are done, the workshop can take place over a one-week period, requiring about two hours per day. The workshop, tested successfully with a Grade 4–5 class, is suitable for Grades 2 to 6. All of the activities suggested can be adapted for your classroom.

Storytelling Plan 1

Selected Text: *The Name of the Tree,* retold by Celia Barker Lottridge

This Bantu tale recounts the search of a group of animals to find food. What they ultimately find is a tree whose fruit is much too high for them to reach. Their survival depends not on who is strongest or smartest but on who can remember and persevere.

This story is appropriate for Kindergarten to secondary levels.

Introducing storytelling

Ask students what they think storytelling is and how it differs from story reading. Prompt them to notice that a storyteller does not read from a book, but tells a story by heart while looking directly at the audience. Ask: "If there is no book, where do the pictures come from?" Brainstorm, and record responses.

Model storytelling with a personal anecdote, and leave time for responses.

Set up brief storytelling warm-up activities, such as the four suggested below, to demonstrate that everyone is a storyteller. Before students break into small groups, identify and practise stop-and-start cues so that everyone gets a turn. Encourage students to participate in one or more activities with a partner or in a small group.

Favorite Place Stories: Arrange students in partners or in circles of 4 or 5. Direct them to describe aloud their favorite place, including as much detail as possible so that the listeners can imagine themselves in that place. Ask for volunteers to perform their story for the whole group. A sample favorite place telling:

> My favorite place is the big rock behind our house. I sit there by myself to think. It is grey and silver and gets warm in the sun . . .

Foolish Things I've Done: Model the telling of such a story (see "The Most Foolish Thing I've Ever Done," page 122). Discuss being dared and doing dangerous things. Direct students to form groups of about four. Encourage them to tell their own stories of foolish things done. Here are a few topics students have spoken about:

- riding a bike right into the creek

- eating a fake cookie meant for the Christmas tree

- trying to hide a dog under a bed

Object Stories: Start off this activity by reaching into a bag without looking, picking up an object, thinking about it, and telling a story. Students then meet in story circles, each with a treasure chest or magic bag of objects to pass around. Each person tells a short tale that the object pulled calls to mind. ("This stone reminds me of the time . . .") Encourage students to tell a personal story or a familiar tale based on the object pulled (e.g., a stone, a feather, a coin); they might even tell their story *to* the object, if cautious.

Name Stories: In preparation, ask students to find out how or why they were given their names or nicknames. Organize students into groups of six, where each person tells a story about his or her name. You may also want to invite parents or grandparents to school to tell stories about how they were named or for whom they were named.

Listening to a story

Set the scene by engaging in a brief visualization exercise. Encourage students to close their eyes as you say: "In your mind's eye, picture a tree. Imagine the look, the smell, and the feel of its leaves, bark, and fruit . . ."

Tell students that you are going to tell them a story called "The Name of the Tree," which has also been treated as a picture book. Ask for predictions or wonder statements based on the title. You might say: "This is a Bantu tale from Africa. What do you wonder about its plot, characters, and setting?" Record the answers and explain that you will return to them later.

Set purposes for listening: Direct the students to listen for the importance of *remembering* in this story. Invite them to join in on the refrain: "Ungali, Ungali, the name of the tree is Ungali," using a drum or rhythm sticks if available.

If the students have not heard a story told in the traditional way without books, props, or pictures, say: "Visualize as you listen. After the story, I will be asking you to tell us what you saw." (You can use the term *visualize* even with very young students as long as you first give examples.) Right after you have told the story, invite students to think about their mental pictures. Prompt them to describe to a partner the scenes they find most vivid.

> In my mind's eye I saw a tall tree with a shiny brown trunk, huge green leaves, and fruits all rainbow-colored, and smelling like apples . . .

Ask for volunteers to describe how they pictured the tree. Encourage detailed descriptions to draw on all five senses. Prompt them to consider the colors of the leaves, the smell and taste of the fruit, the texture of the tree bark, the sound of the leaves rustling, and so on. Discuss the variety of interpretations possible.

After students have described their own scenes, show them the picture book, illustrated by Ian Wallace. Encourage students to compare their initial statements with their present understandings, personal experiences, or familiar folk tales; alternatively, ask them to articulate what they are still wondering about.

Revisiting and responding to a story

The following instructional groupings progress from large group to partner/triad to small group to individual.

Large group

Revisit. Return to the wonder statements recorded before the story was told. Discuss whether students discovered answers while listening and ask what they are still wondering about.

Compare this story with a similar story. For example, other African morality tales include *The Man Who Knew Too Much* by Julius Lester and *The Magic Tree* by Obinkaram Echewa. You may want to create a T-chart with similarities recorded on one side and contrasts, on the other side.

Partner/Triad

Retell the story. Take turns retelling the story from the point of view of one of the characters or of an object in the story, such as a tree in the jungle.

Small group (4–5)

Engage in story drama. Have students re-enact a main event. For example, they can show the animals' trek across the "great flat plain" up to the point where they reach the tree and look up. Tell groups that each person should say one line to help identify the animal he or she is portraying.

Individual/Independent

Draw a picture. Ask students to use pencil crayons to draw the scene from the story they visualized most clearly. Encourage students to draw a key feature such as the tree or a scene such as the animals clustered under the tree.

Making the link between oral storytelling and story writing

Prompt students to write a new version of the story. Direct them to change one element, for example, the setting. In this case, the great flat plain of central Africa might become the forest of Northern Ontario. Tell students to first rehearse their

Story Variation
Once upon a time in Northern Ontario there lived four animals. There was a bunny, and an eagle, and a wolf, and the biggest of all was the King Black Bear. One day they decided to go to the cave that had food and water. They travelled for two days. They finally got to the cave but there was a big rock in front of it. . . .

— Jordyn, age 9

stories with a partner for a designated time (e.g., 10 minutes), switching roles as teller and listener, and providing feedback as directed.

Provide 20 to 30 minutes of uninterrupted writing time, where students write out the stories they have rehearsed as best they remember them. Tell them the wording need not be the same.

Prepare a list of students who want to share their finished stories or works in process with an audience to receive feedback. Emphasize how to offer positive feedback and constructive suggestions. For example, teach **PQP**, where students **praise** specific things about the story, **question** the author about ideas, and offer concrete suggestions on how to **polish** the story. Provide at least 10 minutes for author sharing.

Returning to oral storytelling

Once again, ask students, "What is storytelling?" Record their responses and post them. Work with students to list the steps of how to learn a story for telling (see anchor chart sample on page 127). Post the steps in the storytelling centre, along with a wide assortment of folk tales from anthologies and picture books. "A Selection of Texts for the Telling" on pages 128 to 129 offers ideas. Direct student pairs to work on learning a story. Set a date for students to perform their stories, first in small groups, followed by the whole group.

Creating Digital Stories Together

The model workshop outlined above focuses on traditional storytelling; however, digital storytelling, with its very different approach to visuals, is now an option for students with access to multimedia. We have outlined the experiences of Grade 5–6 teacher Liz McArton, who introduced digital storytelling in the context of her class's daily language and literacy block. She introduced her students to digital storytelling using iMovie and Comic Life. She had access to a mobile Mac lab, but any word-processing program can be used to create exciting digital stories. Her class used colorful graphics with their own artwork and photography, music, and voice in order to create and produce multimedia works. The teaching and learning experiences will be more powerful for yourself and students if you do the following.

1. Learn new technology along with your students, rather than trying to become a full expert before introducing it. This approach provides effective modelling and daily opportunities for interactive learning.
2. Arrange for the students to work in cooperative groupings to create their multimedia artwork, handwritten or typed scripts, and small-group dramatic presentations, which can then be photographed and recorded, and integrated into the final digital stories.
3. Stipulate that no Internet images can be used in the digital stories: the students create their own images through hand-made artwork and/or photography.

Storytelling Plan 2
Focus: To help students make the connection between stories told orally and those digitally created and shared

The following instructional sequence is based on Liz's classroom experiences.
• Use mini-lessons and story models (oral and print) to review story structure (beginning, middle, ending) and story elements (plot, characters, setting, story problem, and solution).

- Model how to create a storyboard to organize the story before recording it. After reading a story aloud, use an interactive whiteboard, if available, to show students how to record the story problem and the main events in sequence.
- Provide a storyboard template and time for constructing stories in storyboard form (cartoon-style boxes using drawings and captions).

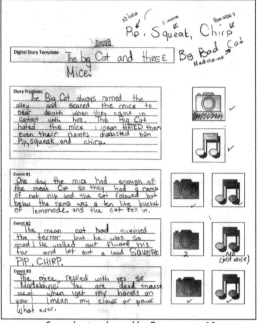

Sample storyboard by Emma, age 10

- Co-construct success criteria with students (see sample below), post them, and refer to them during instructional time.
- Model and guide how to use the storyboard to plan a digital story with visuals and voice narration.
- Provide time and materials for students to illustrate, dramatize, and photograph their stories, as well as support for importing them onto their computers.
- Demonstrate how to use the editing features of the program and have "expert" students demonstrate for their peers.
- Organize presentations of digital stories to classmates, followed by a school-wide Share Fair to which families and the community can be invited.

These are the success criteria that Liz McArton co-constructed with her students, posted, and referred to during instructional time.

Success Criteria

☐ My story has a beginning, middle and ending, with a problem, solution, and clear events that lead to the solution. I have included interesting details to develop my plot.

☐ My titles, transitions, music, and sound effects enhance my story. They are not overpowering or distracting.

☐ My photos/artwork match my story and clearly support the storyline of my script.

☐ My voice can be heard at an appropriate volume. My reading is smooth and practiced, but not too fast. I have spoken with expression.

☐ I have used my class time wisely. I am working toward my personal best. I am working without too many reminders to stay on task.

Ideas for Promoting Storytelling in the Classroom

- Model storytelling with personal anecdotes and familiar folk tales. Stress that even when telling a simple anecdotal story, the tale should be shaped with a beginning, a middle, and an ending; embellished with as many details as possible; and have dialogue between characters included. Model how to maintain eye contact and how to pace and pause to give your audience time to listen and respond. Don't worry about whether you're an expert storyteller or not.

- Make storytelling an intrinsic part of your literacy workshop; for example, partners can respond to a read-aloud by retelling the story in tandem (taking turns) or telling a related story. Similarly, students can rehearse for writing by telling their stories first to a small group or a partner.

- Create a permanent storytelling centre. Stock it with a variety of short fables and folk tales and writing materials. After teaching students how to learn a story using the 10 steps, post the steps at the centre for small-group, partner, and independent work.

- From time to time, play games that promote storytelling. For example, in Liar's Contest, students sit in a circle (small or large group), counting off in beat to the rhyme. The last person the leader counts off in the rhyme (lid) is It. That student tells a personal story and the group votes on whether they think the story is true (fingers in a *V*) or false (fingers crossed). The teller's goal is to "fool" the listeners by making a true story seem implausible and a false story plausible.

- Co-construct a list of steps for learning to tell a story "by heart." (See the anchor chart below.) Tell students that they should focus on making the story their own, rather than on memorizing words.

Rhyme for Liar's Contest
As I **sat** beneath the **app**le tree
All the apples **fell** on me
Apple pudding, **app**le pie,
Did you ever **tell** a lie?
Yes, you did, you **know** you did,
You **broke** your mother's **tea**pot **lid!**
— Traditional

"The tale is not beautiful if nothing is added. Folktales remain merely dumb until you realize that you are required to complete them yourself, to fill in your own participation."
— Italo Calvino

Ten Steps for Learning a Story: Terry Campbell

1. Choose a story you really like (read lots of them first!).
2. Read the story silently several times, **picturing** the story in your mind as you read.
3. Read the story out loud to your partner.
4. **Visualize**, or picture in your mind, all the details of the story and discuss these with your partner.
5. Create a storyboard, using at least three cartoon boxes, to show the main events of the story with pictures and captions. (You will be using this to help you learn to tell the story.)
6. Tell the story to a partner using your storyboard. Don't worry about using the exact words from the book.
7. Tell the story again, without the storyboard. Remember to visualize as you tell.
8. Reread the story from the book to check for missing parts, or special words and phrases you want to remember.
9. PRACTISE! PRACTISE! PRACTISE!
10. Trust the story and yourself. Tell it to your story circle.

Based on Parr & Campbell, 2007

Managing Assessment Challenges

Many teachers are concerned about the fact that process and performance activities such as storytelling, along with the other arts, can be difficult to assess. Clearly described expectations for each activity, and careful observation of the processes — not just an evaluation of the final product or performance — make assessment manageable.

Many aspects of student participation can be assessed. Criteria for the process, such as story planning and rehearsing, and for performance, such as use of voice, can be negotiated with a class and posted as an anchor chart listing success criteria.

Through careful observation of a student's participation, related literacy skills and abilities can also be evaluated. The ability to successfully retell a story, for example, is a powerful indicator that story structure is becoming internalized. Similarly, using story language and gestures to portray a character are indicators of deep comprehension.

Questions to promote student reflection

As with all meaningful assessment, the ultimate purpose of assessing students in storytelling is to inform future teaching and provide feedback that will encourage further growth. The list of questions below is designed with this dual purpose in mind. You may adopt any of them and have students use them for self-assessment.

- Were there times you told a story by yourself? in partners? in small groups? as a whole class? Which way did you prefer?
- How do you engage the audience? Do you maintain eye contact? Do you use gestures and movement to enhance and not detract from the story?
- Was it easier to tell a story in the first person (*I*) or in the third person (*he, she*)? Why?
- Is it necessary to memorize a story in order to tell it? Why do you think that? Is the process the same as learning lines from a script?
- Is a storyteller an actor? Why do you think that? Why do you think storytelling is one of the oldest forms of theatre?

> **Literacy Essential 10:** Storytelling — traditional and digital — allows a teller and an audience to co-create a story using the spoken word and the picture-making ability of the imagination; it thereby provides a key way for students to consolidate their understanding of story and to convey stories that matter to them.

A Selection of Texts for the Telling

The following include traditional and modern folk tales suited to storytelling because of their clear story structure. The beginning, middle, and ending are well sequenced. There is a definite statement of problem and solution, and the characters are easy to relate to.

Involving Families in Storytelling

Storytelling Bag: Have children create a storytelling bag with photos and items from home at the beginning of the year. The items in these bags will be used to help spark storytelling and story-writing ideas.

Family Stories: Invite caregivers, parents, and family members into the classroom to tell their stories along with the children. *Note:* These stories and images can be used to create digital stories.

A sampling of folk tales for telling

Something from Nothing by Phoebe Gilman
The Wolf of Gubbio by Michael Bedard
The Trial of the Stone by Richardo Keens-Douglas
The Name of the Tree by Celia Barker Lottridge
Knots on a Counting Rope by Bill Martin Jr. and John Archambault
The Bone Talker by Shelley A. Leedahl
The Rough-Face Girl by Rafe Martin
Yeh-Shen: A Cinderella Story from China retold by Ai-Ling Louie
Anansi and the Moss-Covered Rock by Eric A. Kimmel
The Three Billy Goats Gruff by P. C. Asbjornsen and J. E. Moe

Traditional literature anthologies for storytelling and drama

Canadian Fairy Tales edited by Eva Martin and Laszlo Gal
English Fairy Tales collected by Joseph Jacobs
Fables edited by Arnold Lobel
The Magic Orange Tree edited by Diane Wolkstein
Favorite Folktales from Around the World edited by Jane Yolen
Out of the Everywhere: New Tales for Canada edited by Jan Andrews and
    Simon Ng

FINAL THOUGHTS

Charting New Worlds

I'm not a teacher: only a fellow traveller of whom you asked the way. I pointed ahead — ahead of myself as well as you.
— George Bernard Shaw

Teachers have many roles to fulfill, particularly as we move forward into a world of increasingly complex and multimodal texts. The roles we fulfill every day in our classrooms as captain, purposeful traveller, map reader, and chartmaker will continue to be critical components of our practice in the future. But as we find ourselves juggling multiple maps, we realize that the maps of the future will be far more diverse, offering so many more opportunities for exploration and navigation.

Here, we have mapped out the possibilities of what we consider to be our 10 literacy essentials. Perhaps it is surprising that, in addition to reading, writing, and talk, we chose to emphasize the importance of understanding yourself, your students, and your students' families, community building, poetry, drama, and storytelling, apparently on an equal footing. In so doing, we as teachers and travellers are expressing our belief that it is vital for literacy learners to explore and discover, both on their own and with fellow travellers, in order to courageously chart and navigate today's texts. Just as important, we want learners to discover through their strengths, the comfort and confidence required to navigate the unexplored and potentially challenging maps of their futures. To become skilled and strategic navigators, learners require diverse opportunities in the classroom and in their worlds to encounter, use, and create texts of many types and formats. As they chart their routes, they will need to be ever mindful of travellers they may encounter along the way.

As we look towards future adventures, we envision times when our students will know at least as much as, if not more than, we do about certain things. We acknowledge our status as fellow travellers and collaborators, co-constructing knowledge as we explore and learn together. And we know that our ultimate task will be to know when, where, and how to hang up our hats as captains and shift responsibility to students, allowing them to read their environments, chart their courses, and navigate independently and successfully a sea of words and oceans of texts. Along with Frederick the field mouse, let's gather our supplies of words, colors, and dreams, and embark on voyages to destinations we can only imagine.

The Literacy Essentials as Presented in This Book

1. For your literacy journey in the classroom, adopt the adventurous orientation of a navigator, critically aware of personal strengths, formative influences, and dimensions that need to be considered.
2. A classroom community founded on clear routines, knowledge of students, respect, and conscious use of community-building activities makes possible the effective teaching of literacy curriculum.
3. A workshop structure with warm-ups, mini-lessons, independent study, centre activities, and conferences combines theory and practice and enables students and teachers to develop independently and collaboratively as navigators of literacy.
4. Given the fact that talk is the foundation of literacy learning, promote accountable talk through explicit teaching and modelling, emphasizing that students interact with one another with respect, attentive listening, and an openness to new ideas.
5. Reading aloud every day to every child a "just right" text that you enjoy and use to prompt critical thinking provides an excellent way to model literate behaviors; students can then follow your modelling to further develop as literate beings.
6. The teaching of reading begins with an understanding that students need to read not only the words before them but the world around them. It demands use of a full continuum of support, beginning with modelling, encompassing guided work in small groups, and leading to opportunities for students to show reader independence. It also recognizes that making meaning of a text can be a collaborative effort.
7. To write is to put one's mark on the world in a way that invites the reader to come closer. To help students make connections between reading and writing and to teach and assess writing, use mentor texts and real-life experiences in ways that allow students to be travellers of the world of text.
8. Children need poetry! Use poetry, with all its oral appeal and liberating potential, to engage students in playing with and exploring language, both aloud and written.
9. As a dynamic form of learning, drama belongs squarely in the classroom. When you infuse role-taking and drama strategies into your teaching, student engagement will deepen, and you can better bring stories and information to life. Diverse students can use drama as scaffolding to develop further as readers and writers.
10. Storytelling — traditional and digital — allows a teller and an audience to co-create a story using the spoken word and the picture-making ability of the imagination; it thereby provides a key way for students to consolidate their understanding of story and to convey stories that matter to them.

Navigating the Dimensions Involved in Teaching Language and Literacy

Check and provide examples to help deepen your awareness of what is happening in your language and literacy block.

The Instructional Dimension: *Constructing learning experiences using what are traditionally referred to as the six language arts, texts of many types, multiple levels of support, and diverse teaching/learning strategies*

Characteristics	Classroom Examples

Six Language Arts:

☐ Listening:

☐ Speaking:

☐ Reading:

☐ Writing:

☐ Viewing:

☐ Representing:

Texts of Many Types and Formats

☐ Oral texts:

☐ Multimedia texts:

☐ Technology-mediated texts:

☐ Multiple levels of texts:

☐ Student choice of texts:

☐ Literacy texts:

☐ Content/Information texts:

☐ Other:

Pembroke Publishers © 2012 *Balanced Literacy Essentials* by Michelann Parr, Terry Campbell. ISBN 978-1-55138-275-3

Teaching/Learning Strategies

☐ Continuum of support, with gradual release of responsibility:

☐ Range of instructional strategies (e.g., student-centred, cooperative):

☐ Student groupings (independent, small/ large group):

☐ Organizational structures (e.g., anchor charts, workshops, literacy centres):

☐ Diverse assessment tools (e.g., checklist, conference, rubric, negotiated success criteria, portfolio):

The Individual Dimension: *Shaping your teaching by taking into account how individuals learn and navigate texts of many types*

Characteristics	Classroom Examples
Multiple Intelligences	
☐ Linguistic (word smart):	
☐ Logical-mathematical (number/ reasoning smart):	
☐ Spatial (picture smart):	
☐ Bodily-Kinesthetic (body smart):	
☐ Musical (music smart):	
☐ Interpersonal (people smart)	
☐ Intrapersonal (self smart):	
☐ Naturalist (nature smart):	

Pembroke Publishers © 2012 *Balanced Literacy Essentials* by Michelann Parr, Terry Campbell. ISBN 978-1-55138-275-3

Ways of Knowing

☐ Listening:

☐ Observing:

☐ Doing, constructing, investigating:

☐ Reflecting on experience:

☐ Thinking abstractly:

Ways of Being

☐ Culture:

☐ Family characteristics:

The Real-World Dimension: *Building bridges between the classroom and the realities of everyday life in the 21st century*

Characteristics	Classroom Examples

Critical Literacy

☐ Looking at the familiar in fresh, critical ways:

☐ Closely considering multiple viewpoints/ perspectives:

☐ Travelling purposefully in the world of text:

☐ Charting new courses:

REFERENCES

Allen, J. (2002). *On the same page: Shared reading beyond the primary grades.* Portland, ME: Stenhouse.

Arquette, C. (2006). Multiple activity literacy centres: Promoting choice and learning differentiation. *Illinois Reading Council Journal, 35*(3), 3–9.

Booth, D. (2005). *Story drama: Creating stories through role play, improvising, and reading aloud* (2nd ed.). Markham, ON: Pembroke.

Booth, D., & Barton, B. (2000). *Story works.* Markham, ON: Pembroke.

Booth, D., & Lundy, C. J. (1985). *Improvisation: Learning through drama.* Toronto, ON: Harcourt Brace Jovanovich.

Booth, D., & Moore, B. (1988). *Poems please! Sharing poetry with children.* Markham, ON: Pembroke.

Calkins, L. (1986, 1994). *The art of teaching writing.* Portsmouth, NH: Heinemann.

Calkins, L., & Harwayne, S. (1987). *The writing workshop: A world of difference.* Portsmouth, NH: Heinemann.

Cambourne, B. (2000/01). Conditions for literacy learning. *Reading Teacher, 54*(4), 414–417.

Cambourne, B. (2001). What do I do with the rest of the class? The nature of teaching–learning activities. *Language Arts, 79*(2), 124–135.

Campbell, T., & Hlusek, M. (2009). Storytelling and story writing: Using a different kind of pencil (Research Monograph No. 20). *What Works? Research into Practice.* Retrieved from the Literacy and Numeracy Secretariat website: www.edu.gov.on.ca/eng/literacynumeracy/inspire/research/whatWorks.html

Christensen, L. (2004). Warriors don't cry: Acting for justice. *Rethinking Schools, 18*(3), 48–50.

Clay, M. (1998). *By different paths to common outcomes.* York, ME: Stenhouse.

Clay, M. (2000). *Running records for classroom teachers.* Portsmouth, NH: Heinemann.

Clay, M. (2002, 2006). *An observation survey of early literacy achievement.* Portsmouth, NH: Heinemann.

Clay, M. (2004). Talking, reading, and writing. *Journal of Reading Recovery, 3*(2), 1–15.

Clyde, J. A. (2003). Stepping inside the story world: The subtext strategy: A tool for connecting and comprehending. *Reading Teacher, 57*(2), 150–160.

Commeyras, M., Bisplinghoff, B. S., & Olsen, J. (2003). *Teachers as readers: Perspectives on the importance of reading in teachers' classrooms and lives.* Newark, NJ: International Reading Association.

Cornett, C. E., & Smithrim, K. L. (2001). *The arts as meaning makers: Integrating literature and the arts throughout the curriculum* (Canadian ed.). Toronto, ON: Prentice-Hall.

Cremin, T. (2009). Creative teachers and creative teaching. In A. Wilson (Ed.), *Creativity in primary education* (2nd ed.) (pp. 36–46). Achieving QTS Cross-Curricular Strand. Exeter, UK: Learning Matters.

Cremin, T., Mottram, M., Collins, F., & Powell, S. (2011). *Building communities of readers.* Leicester, UK: United Kingdom Literacy Association (UKLA).

Cunningham, P., & Allington, R. (2006). *Classrooms that work: They can all read and write* (4th ed.). Boston, MA: Allyn & Bacon.

Cunningham, P., & Allington, R. (2010). *Classrooms that work: They can all read and write* (5th ed.). Boston, MA: Allyn & Bacon.

Daniels, H. (2002). *Literature circles: Voice and choice in book clubs and reading groups.* York, ME: Stenhouse.

Day, J. P., Spiegel, D. L., McLellan, J., & Brown, V. B. (2002). *Moving forward with literature circles.* New York, NY: Scholastic.

Denton, C. A., Ciancio, D., & Fletcher, J. (2006). Validity, reliability, and utility of the observation survey of early literacy achievement. *Reading Research Quarterly, 41,* 8–34.

Diller, D. (2008). *Spaces and places: Designing classrooms for literacy.* Portland, ME: Stenhouse.

Durkin, D. (2004). *Teaching them to read.* Boston, MA: Allyn & Bacon.

Fish, S. (2011). *How to write a sentence: And how to read one.* New York, NY: HarperCollins.

Fletcher, R. (1996). *Breathing in breathing out: Keeping a writer's notebook.* Portsmouth, NH: Heinemann.

Ford, M. P., & Opitz, M. F. (2002). Using centers to engage children during guided reading time: Intensifying learning experiences away from the teacher. *Reading Teacher, 55*(8), 710–717.

Fountas, I. C., & Pinnell, G. S. (1996). *Guided reading: Good first teaching for all children.* Portsmouth, NH: Heinemann.

Fountas, I. C., & Pinnell, G. S. (2001). *Guiding readers and writers (Grades 3–6).* Portsmouth, NH: Heinemann.

Fountas, I., & Pinnell, G. S. (2001). Classroom management videotapes: *Managing the day, planning for effective teaching.* Portsmouth, NH: Heinemann.

Gardner, H. (1999). *Intelligence reframed: Multiple intelligences for the 21st century.* New York, NY: Basic Books.

Graves, D. (1994). *A fresh look at writing.* Portsmouth, NH: Heinemann.

Graves, D., & Kittle, P. (2005). *Inside writing.* Portsmouth, NH: Heinemann.

Harrison, D. L., & Holderith, K. (2003). *Using the power of poetry to teach language arts, social studies, math, and more: Engaging poetry lessons, model poems, and writing activities that help students learn important content.* New York, NY: Scholastic.

Harwayne, S. (2001). *Writing through childhood: Rethinking process and product.* Portsmouth, NH: Heinemann.

Johnson, L., & O'Neill, C. (Eds.). (1984). *Dorothy Heathcote: Collected writings on education and drama.* London, UK: Hutchison.

Keene, E. O., & Zimmerman, S. (1997). *Mosaic of thought: Teaching comprehension in a readers' workshop.* Portsmouth, NH: Heinemann.

Lakoff, G., & Johnson, M. (1980). *Metaphors we live by.* Chicago, IL: University of Chicago Press.

Laman, T. T. (2006). Changing our minds/Changing the world: The power of a question. *Language Arts, 83*(3), 203–214.

Leland, C., Harste, J., & Helt, C. (2000). Multiple ways of knowing: Lessons from a blue guitar. In M. A. Gallago & S. Hollingsworth (Eds.), *What counts as literacy: Challenging the school standard* (pp. 106–117). New York, NY: Teachers College Press.

Massengill-Shaw, D. M., & Mahlios, M. (2011). Literacy metaphors of pre-service teachers: Do they change after instruction? Which metaphors are stable? How do they connect to theories? *Journal of Education for Teaching, 37*(1): 77–92.

Ontario Ministry of Education. (2006). *A guide to effective literacy instruction.* Grades 4–6. Access online at: http://www.eworkshop.on.ca

Ontario Ministry of Education. (2010–2011). *The full-day early learning Kindergarten program.* Retrieved from the Ministry of Education's website: http://www.edu.gov.on.ca

Owocki, G. (1999). *Literacy through play.* Portsmouth, NH: Heinemann.

Owocki, G. (2001). *Make way for literacy! Teaching the way young children learn.* Portsmouth, NH: Heinemann.

Paley, V. (1997). *The girl with the brown crayon.* Cambridge, MA: Harvard University Press.

Parr, M. (2011). The voice of text-to-speak technology: One possible solution for struggling readers? *What Works? Research into Practice* (Research Monograph No. 35). Retrieved from Literacy and Numeracy Secretariat http://www.edu.gov.on.ca/eng/literacynumeracy/inspire/research/whatWorks

Parr, M., & Campbell, T. (2007). *Teaching the language arts: Engaging literacy practices.* Toronto, ON: Wiley & Sons.

Rasinski, T. (2006). Moving beyond accuracy, automaticity, and prosody. *The Reading Teacher, 59*(7), 704–706.

Routman, R. (2000). *Conversations: Strategies for teaching, learning and evaluating.* Portsmouth, NH: Heinemann.

Routman, R. (2005). *Writing essentials: Raising expectations and results while simplifying teaching.* Portsmouth, NH: Heinemann.

Rubin, D. L. (1990). Introduction: Ways of talking about talking and learning. In S. Hynds & D. L. Rubin (Eds.), *Perspectives on talk and learning* (pp. 1–17). Urbana, IL: National Council of Teachers of English.

Swartz, L. (2002). *The new dramathemes.* Markham, ON: Pembroke.

Swartz, L., & Nyman, D. (2010). *Drama themes, schemes, & dreams.* Markham, ON: Pembroke.

Taberski, S. (2000). *On solid ground: Strategies for teaching reading K–3.* Portsmouth, NH: Heinemann.

Vasquez, V. M. (2001). *Getting beyond "I like the book": Creating space for critical literacy in K–6 classrooms.* Newark, DE: International Reading Association.

Vygotsky, L. S. (1978). *Mind in society.* Cambridge, MA: Harvard University Press.

Wells, G. (2003). Children talk their way into literacy (Los niños se alfabetizan hablando). In J. R. Garcia (Ed.), Enseñar a escribir sin prisas . . . pero con sentido. (Santa Cruz, CA: University of California). Retrieved from people.ucsc.edu/~gwells/Files/Papers_Folder/Talk-Literacy.pdf

INDEX